Praise for *The Naked Presenter*

"Many books about presentation delivery cover simple topics like eye contact and gestures. Garr's book goes much deeper, highlighting Zen concepts that address meaningful ways to connect credibly with an audience. It's a must-read for anyone who has to give presentations."

—**Nancy Duarte**, CEO of Duarte Design and author of *slide:ology* and *resonate*

"You can capture the essence of Garr and his work in three words: beauty/logic/Asia. A true original, and a voice worth listening to."

—**Seth Godin**, author of *Linchpin*

"I do between 80 and 100 speaking events per year. That's a full-time job in and of itself, but it's a sure-fire business development tool for our agency. The only reason this model works so well for us is because I take everything Garr Reynolds says to heart. I don't read his books, I devour them from the inside out. From the structure of the presentation to how to make the slides brilliant, nobody beats Garr. *The Naked Presenter* is a book whose time has come. Shedding everything to focus on the audience and the content is the true secret to great presentations. Now, Garr is sharing that secret (and how to do it) with the world. Thank you, Garr!"

—**Mitch Joel**, president of Twist Image and author of *Six Pixels of Separation*

"You've probably watched a TED Talk, or seen someone who just owns the stage like Tom Peters and has the audience gasping for more, but did you know that you too can deliver presentations that get great reviews? You can by being a Naked Presenter. I've used these techniques to be a better presenter and they work. Use them and your audience will rave about your presentations. Heck, they might even stop Twittering during your presentations. Imagine that."

—**Robert Scoble**, video blogger, technical evangelist, and coauthor of *Naked Conversations*

The
naked **presenter**

Delivering Powerful Presentations With or Without Slides

Garr Reynolds

**New
Riders**

VOICES THAT MATTER™

The Naked Presenter
Delivering Powerful Presentations With or Without Slides
Garr Reynolds

New Riders
1249 Eighth Street
Berkeley, CA 94710
510/524-2178
Fax: 510/524-2221

Find us on the Web at www.newriders.com
To report errors, please send a note to errata@peachpit.com
New Riders is an imprint of Peachpit, a division of Pearson Education
Copyright © 2011 by Garr Reynolds

Senior Editor: Karyn Johnson
Production Editor: Hilal Sala
Copy Editor: Kelly Kordes Anton
Compositor: Kim Scott, Bumpy Design
Proofreader: Elizabeth Welch
Indexer: Valerie Haynes Perry
Design Consultants: Mayumi Nakamoto, Mimi Heft
Book and Cover Design: Garr Reynolds

ISBN-13: 978-0-321-70445-0
ISBN-10:   0-321-70445-2

9 8 7 6 5 4 3 2 1

Printed and bound in the United States of America

To Mom

Ruth Louise Reynolds (1927–2010)

Contents

Acknowledgments

There are a lot of people I'd like to thank for their help: my great editor, Karyn Johnson, for her fantastic suggestions and unbelievable patience; Mimi Heft for her help with the design; Hilal Sala, production editor, for her talent and great patience; Kim Scott for her help with the layout; and Sara Jane Todd for her wonderful marketing efforts.

Thanks to Nancy Duarte and Mark Duarte and all the wonderful staff at Duarte Design in Silicon Valley, including Paula Tesch and Krystin Brazie, for their support.

Thanks to Seth Godin, Mitch Joel, Robert Scoble, and Guy Kawasaki for the kind words and inspiration. Thanks to Deryn Verity, Keiji Enomoto, and Davide Giglio for their enlightened advice. Thanks to Jumpei Matsuoka and all the cool people at iStockphoto.com for their tremendous support with the images and the special offer that's included at the back of this book, and to designer Mayumi Nakamoto for always being there when I needed her.

A special thanks to Chris Craft, Pam Slim, Phil Waknell, and Les Posen for their very kind contributions. A big thank-you to those who contributed ideas and inspiration, including Debbie Thorn, CZ Robertson, Ric Bretschneider, and Howard and Rachel Cooperstein. And to Mark and Liz Reynolds for the great pad at the beach.

To the business and design community in Japan, including Shigeki Yamamoto, Tom Perry, Darren Saunders, Daniel Rodriguez, David Baldwin, Nathan Bryan, Jiri Mestecky, Doug Schafer, Barry Louie, Michael Bobrove, Daniel Kwintner, Keizo Yamada, and Yuko Nakaoka. To Patrick Newell in Tokyo for his contributions and friendship.

Thank you to Reiko Hiromoto at Kansai Gaidai University for her insights and suggestions. And thanks to Maho Fujino and all the staff at the local Starbucks in Japan for their friendly smiles everyday.

I'd like to thank the thousands of subscribers to the Presentation Zen blog and to all the blog readers who have contacted me over the years to share their stories and examples, including Olivia Mitchell, Mike Brown, and Natasha Lampard in New Zealand.

And of course I am indebted to my wife and daughter in Japan for making me laugh everyday.

To express yourself as you are is
the most important thing.

— Shunryu Suzuki

1

Naturalness and the Art of Presenting Naked

I had only been living in Japan a couple of months when I found myself sitting outside in a large and very hot Japanese bath surrounded by my naked coworkers. I was at an *onsen* (温泉), or Japanese hot springs, along with everyone else from my office, as part of our company weekend retreat. The purpose of the trip was not work, but simply relaxation, dining, drinking, and a little fun with colleagues. By getting away from the formality of the office setting, my boss told me, staff and managers can experience a more natural and spontaneous form of communication and build better relationships that will be good for business in the long term. Eating and drinking are part of the onsen experience, and so is communal nude bathing, which is thought to strengthen bonds among team members. This is when I first learned the phrase *hadaka no tsukiai* (裸の付き合い), which means naked relationship or naked communication. My boss informed me that the Japanese bath is an important part of the Japanese way of life, and the ritual itself is also a good metaphor for healthy communication and good relationships. Through mutual nakedness we are all the same, he said, regardless of rank. When you remove the formalities and the barriers and go naked, communication improves and people and their ideas connect. With hadaka no tsukiai, to soak with others in your in-group is to freely expose yourself and communicate the "naked truth." The spirit behind this kind of exposure leads to better, more honest communication. This same spirit can be applied to presentations as well.

Who Is This Book For?

This book is for anyone who has a deep desire to improve their presentations by seriously increasing the level of engagement they create with an audience. Many people need to stand up and make presentations, but this book is specifically designed for people who may already be comfortable designing visuals yet still have a deep desire to refine their delivery skills and ability to connect with an audience.

My approach to presentations embraces the tenets of restraint, simplicity, and naturalness. Though all three of these tenets are important in every aspect of the presentation process, restraint and simplicity are especially important in the preparation of your message and the design of your visuals.

My first two books—*Presentation Zen* and *Presentation Zen Design*—focused on preparation and design. This book focuses on delivery after touching briefly on issues related to preparation. Inspired by the Japanese onsen and the idea of hadaka no tsukiai—hence the title *The Naked Presenter*—and the Japanese Zen aesthetic that places great importance on learning from nature, the underlying theme of this book is naturalness. The simple ideas in this book are designed to help you make natural connections with your audience and deliver powerful presentations that are effective and remembered.

Naturally Naked

It may not seem like it sometimes in the ultra-modern, fast-paced urban centers like Tokyo or Osaka, but nature, or *shizen* (自然), plays a central role in Japanese culture. The outdoor hot springs bath is a time for relaxation, contemplation, and connecting with the natural surroundings outside the bath. In this environment one feels a naturalness that is nothing short of liberating. The Zen scholar Daisetz Suzuki (1870–1966) often discussed the deep affection the Japanese have for nature and how the yearning for that connection was something deep in all of us. "However 'civilized,' however much brought up in an artificially contrived environment," Suzuki said, "we all seem to have an innate longing for primitive simplicity, close to the natural state of living."

This desire for nature or more naturalness does not mean that we hope to return to a primitive time of ancient generations, but simply that we yearn for more natural freedom of expression, an immediacy, and a sense of being earnestly connected to our environment and to others. We can apply the spirit of this yearning for naturalness to our professional lives today as well. When it comes to communicating in today's "civilized," high-tech environments, for example, we still innately long for a kind of primitive simplicity in which our interactions with others have a deeper sense of naturalness, freedom, and spontaneity. We want clear instructions, meaningful data, illustrative stories, and frank conversations. Yet too often we get vague language, obfuscation, and dense decks of PowerPoint slides instead of understanding and meaningful connections.

Presentations and naturalness

Presentation technology has evolved over the years, but this does not mean presentations have necessarily evolved much. "Death by PowerPoint" is still too common. Thanks to the work of communication experts such as Bert Decker, Jerry Weissman, and Carmine Gallo, and presentation design gurus such as Nancy Duarte and Cliff Atkinson—plus many more around the world—things have improved. Progress is being made, and while presentation techniques have changed as digital technology has progressed, the fundamentals of what makes an effective presentation today are essentially the same as they ever were, and naturalness in delivery remains a key.

This naturalness is not something that can be forced. "To be truly effective," says the legendary Dale Carnegie, "you must speak with such intensified and exalted naturalness that your auditors will never dream that you have been trained." No matter how much you train, or how extensively you use digital tools in live presentations, tools and techniques must be used only to clarify, simplify, and support the personal connection that develops between an audience and a speaker. Technology and the latest tools can be great enablers and amplifiers of your messages, but they must be used wisely and with restraint in a way that feels natural and real—otherwise they become barriers to communication.

Technology and all that jazz

There are many similarities between the art of jazz and the art of presentation in all its myriad forms. Jazz is complex and it's deep but also simple and accessible. Jazz makes the complex simple through profound expressions of clarity and sincerity. It has structure and rules—but within those constraints, it also offers great freedom. Above all, jazz is natural. Whether we are talking about public speaking or playing music, communication and connection always transcend the tools involved. Wynton Marsalis, the American jazz trumpeter and composer, reminds us that while technology is great it is only a tool. In a 2009 Authors@Google Talk, Marsalis said this about technology and jazz:

> I don't think we should feel that because our tools have become more advanced, we are more advanced. The technology of the soul has not changed for a long time. Many times we use technological advances to stand in for we are more advanced. Jazz is not like that. You can come up with all the synthesizers you want, it's still not going to be able to swing.... This music celebrates human beings and our creativity.
>
> —Wynton Marsalis

With presentations, too, remember that no matter how impressive the technology becomes, no matter how many features and effects are added, the technology of the soul, as Marsalis put it, has indeed not changed. Technologies such as PowerPoint and Keynote—or new tools like Prezi—are only useful to the degree that they amplify our message, make things clearer and more memorable, and strengthen the human-to-human connection that is the basis of communication. Used well, multimedia has the power to do this. But too often presentations given with the help of multimedia suffer because the presenter puts too much energy and emphasis on the technology or visuals and not enough on making a meaningful connection with the audience.

Whether it's making a presentation or playing music, sincerity and connection are more important than tools. (Photo by Nikolas Papageorgiou.)

What Does It Mean to Present Naked?

At its core, presenting naked means connecting and engaging with an audience, whether three people or three thousand, in a way that is direct, honest, and clear. Naked means putting your audience first. It means being transparent and taking a chance by allowing yourself to be vulnerable and exposed. Being naked involves stripping away all that is unnecessary to get at the essence of your message. The naked approach embraces the ideas of simplicity, integrity, and passion. The approach feels fresh—perhaps even a bit cheeky—and far more satisfying to both presenter and audience as your true, natural personality shines through.

One who presents naked feels free. Free from worry. Free from anxiety over what other people may or may not think. Free from self-doubt. Free from tricks and gimmicks and the pressure to pull those off. Free from hiding behind anything (including slides) and the fear of possible exposure that accompanies such hiding. A naked presenter removes all encumbrances, is totally in the moment, and engages with the audience. And if multimedia is used it fits well within the talk and is harmonious with the message. Simple, well-designed visuals are in sync yet never steal the show or rise above serving a strong, supportive role that helps engage the audience.

Presenting naked and naturally is hard to do because we're not in the habit. But it wasn't always this way. When we were younger and we performed "show and tell" at the front of the class in elementary school, we were honest and engaged—sometimes our candor even made the other children laugh and the teacher blush. But it was real. We told great stories—and we were only six. Now we are experienced and mature, we have advanced degrees and deep knowledge in important fields—and we are boring. One reason we are so dull as adult presenters is because we are overly cautious. We are afraid. We want everything all to be so safe and perfect, so we overthink things and put up a great many barriers. We're afraid so we retreat, however unconsciously, and play it safe by hiding behind a stack of bulleted lists in a darkened room in a style void of emotion. After all, no one ever got fired for just providing information, right? But if your audience is asleep, or if they tune you out, your list of information serves no purpose.

Think conversation not performance

It is tempting to think of presentations like a performance. Often you're on a stage under lights and standing in front of a group of people waiting for you to deliver the goods. However, while there are some things you can learn from performers—such as dealing with nerves and projecting your voice and so on—it is much better to view the art of presentation like a conversation. Earlier I mentioned that the art of presentation has many parallels with the art of jazz. But aren't jazz musicians performing when they play? Most people would say they are, but jazz as a musical art form is also much more like a conversation—as it requires of a musician great empathy and the ability to listen well. Wynton Marsalis calls jazz "The music of dialogue."

Although you may be on stage and the center of attention, think of your talk as more of a conversation than a performance.

Most communication experts today agree that a good talk or a good presentation should feel more like a conversation. Granville Toogood, a respected executive communications coach, suggests the conversational approach rather than a performance of speech-like delivery. "Stop thinking that every time you stand up to say something you are making a speech—because you're not," says Toogood in *The Articulate Executive* (McGraw-Hill, 1996). "What you are really doing is having an enlarged conversation." In *The Power Presenter* (Wiley, 2009), presentation coach Jerry Weissman also discusses the importance of presenting in a manner that is more like a conversation than a performance. Here again the emphasis is not on teaching people how to become performers (which 99 percent of us are not), but rather on helping them to become more *natural* presenters. As Weissman says early in the book while talking about his coaching career, "My goal was to move the businesspeople I coached to become successful presenters naturally."

Think of your presentation as a "large conversation" instead of a performance or speech.

Natural expression of yourself

Naturalness in delivery, then, should not be a formal, one-way didactic lecture. Rather, imagine the delivery of your presentation as a conversation between friends or coworkers, teacher and student, a master and apprentice, or scientist to scientist. They all involve personal connection by way of natural expression. You'll find something parallel to this kind of thinking in Shunryu Suzuki's *Zen Mind, Beginner's Mind* (Weatherhill, 1973) in a small section on communication. This passage hints at the point I'm making about naturalness in the context of presentation:

> *In Zen we put emphasis on demeanor, or behavior. By behavior we do not mean a particular way that you ought to behave, but rather the natural expression of yourself. We emphasize straightforwardness. You should be true to your feelings, and to your mind, expressing yourself without any reservations. This helps the listener to understand more easily.*
>
> *—Shunryu Suzuki*

You can apply these simple ideas about Zen and communication to your everyday presentations as well as meetings, networking events, and so on. That is, the emphasis should be on the natural expression of yourself, honesty, and straightforwardness, rather than on following a memorized script of the "right way" to behave or the "correct way" to present. As Suzuki says, "Without any intentional, fancy way of adjusting yourself, to express yourself as you are is the most important thing."

Phil Waknell

Phil Waknell is an inspirational speaker, writer, and presentation coach. He is cofounder of Ideas on Stage, the leading Paris-based presentation specialists, a company he runs with his business partner Pierre Morsa.

www.ideasonstage.com

Here Phil shares his tips on presenting, likening the naked approach to a samurai removing his armor and laying down his weapon.

Presenting Naked

A samurai would go into battle armed with a sword and wearing armor. Fighting "naked" would mean hand-to-hand combat with no protection. Presenting naked is about taking off your armor, putting down your sword and shield, and facing your audience "man to man," as it were. It's about removing anything that is there only for the benefit of the presenter, and not for the benefit of the audience. It's about being authentic, being true—being you.

Break down the barriers
You need to make a connection with your audience. It's hard to connect when you stay at a distance or behind barriers. For example, don't stand behind a lectern. It just accentuates the feeling of "I'm up here, you're down there." What you really want to do is communicate WITH your audience not just talk AT them (or, worse, talk DOWN TO them). Get close to your audience. If you can reasonably walk among them while still making yourself heard, then do so from time to time.

Lay down your weapons
A fighter attempts to win by hitting his opponent—hard. Likewise, many presenters hit the audience with a flurry of facts and bludgeon them into submission.

Presenting naked means putting down your weapons and realizing that your aim is not to persuade people that you are right and they are wrong. That is a temporary achievement. Sure, it's easy to bombard the audience with facts, but it's not effective—and if you don't aim to communicate effectively, you shouldn't be presenting at all.

Start not from what *you* know, but from where the audience is. If you need to change their minds, help them realize they need to change their thinking. It needs to be their thought processes that trigger the change. Connect with the audience, show them a new direction, and help them want to explore it.

Remove your armor

Perhaps the hardest part of presenting naked is taking off your armor—your comfort and protection. The first thing to remove is the crutch of referring to notes on your slides. Prepare properly so that you never need to look at the wall behind you. Equally, your slides—if you need any—should be stripped of anything unnecessary. Make them simple and clear, and ensure they are relevant to your message. The next piece of armor to remove is your agenda, the comfort of knowing what comes next. Like a wise samurai who changes plans on the battlefield if his original plan is failing, a presenter needs to be flexible and adapt to the situation and the audience.

Cast off any self-importance. You are not presenting because you are important, but because the audience is important. It's hard to make a connection if you put yourself on a pedestal, literally or figuratively. You're there to communicate, not to impress anyone.

Let go

Finally, let go of your sense of self. You are not there for yourself: You are there for the audience. You have no personal aims or cares other than to communicate your message effectively. You have no worries that people won't like your style. Just be yourself, be authentic, and care deeply about the audience. Trust that the rest will take care of itself. It will.

Don't be boring

One of the keys to a natural, conversational approach includes removing all barriers to natural communication with the audience. These barriers might include reading off notes, standing behind a lectern, failing to make good eye contact, speaking too softly, or using jargon or language that is formal, stiff, or fails to appeal to the audience's emotion and natural curiosity.

Now, some do believe that technical professionals and scientists are necessarily dry, boring speakers, unable to communicate the relevance of their work to the greater public. But this is not so. Richard Feynman, for example, was a brilliant Nobel Prize–winning scientist who was a passionate teacher and communicator, able to engage students and general audiences with great enthusiasm and clarity. Carl Sagan, of course, was known for his ability to talk clearly and passionately about the cosmos. Today, one of my favorite communicators—Neil deGrasse Tyson—is also a scientist. Tyson is an astrophysicist with a great mind, infectious curiosity, and an amazing ability to inspire and inform audiences through his natural, conversational delivery style.

No matter your background or profession—whether you have a technical or scientific background, are in business, teach school, or are a student—there's no excuse for being boring.

Presentation Generation

The ability to stand and deliver a powerful presentation that engages the whole minds of the audience members has never been more important than today. Some have called our modern era "presentation generation." The ability to speak passionately, clearly, and visually is more important today than ever before –partly because of the fantastic reach that our talks can have, largely thanks to the power of online video. What you say and what you present visually today can now be captured easily and cheaply in HD video and broadcast around the world for anyone to see. The potential of your speech or your presentation to change things—maybe even change the world—goes far beyond just the words spoken. Words are important, but if it were just about words, you could create a detailed document, disseminate it, and that would be that. Effective presentations allow you to amplify the meaning of your words.

While speaking about the power of online video to spread innovative ideas at the 2010 TED Global conference in Oxford, England, TED curator Chris Anderson spoke also of the great power of face-to-face communication and presentation to influence change. Anderson underscored the fact that information usually can be taken in faster by reading it. But the necessary depth and richness is often missing. Part of the effectiveness of a presentation is the visual impact and the show-and-tell aspect of it. The presentation visuals and the structure and the story are compelling aspects of a presentation, even a recorded presentation that is posted online. However, as Anderson says, there is much more to it than that:

There's a lot more being transferred than just words. It is in that nonverbal portion that there's some serious magic. Somewhere hidden in the physical gestures, the vocal cadence, the facial expressions, the eye contact, the passion, and the kind of awkward British body language, the sense of how the audience are reacting.... There are hundreds of subconscious clues that go to how well you will understand and whether you are inspired.

—Chris Anderson

We are wired for face-to-face communication, Anderson says. "Face-to-face communication has been fine tuned by millions of years of evolution. That's what's made it into this mysterious powerful thing it is. Someone speaks, and there is resonance in all these receiving brains. [Then] the whole group acts together. This is the connective tissue of the human super organism in action. It has driven our culture for millennia."

In a digital age, remarkable presentations and great ideas can travel fast and be seen by millions.

Raising the bar and making a difference

Over the last few years the state of presentations has gotten better. Many researchers, businesspeople, teachers, and students have seen the light and are creating and delivering presentations that appeal to both logic and emotion. And if they use multimedia or other forms of visuals, they are well thought out and designed according to fundamental design principles, not tired template clichés. Organizations such as TED have proven the value and influence that well-crafted and engaging presentations can have to teach, persuade, and inspire. Progress is being made on the presentation front. However, on the whole, the majority of presentations in business and academia are still mind-numbingly dull, tedious affairs that fail to connect and engage audiences, even though the content may be important.

The bar is still relatively low when it comes to the quality of presentations, especially those given with the aid of multimedia. This is not bad news necessarily—in fact, it is an opportunity. It's an opportunity for you to be different. You have important ideas that are worth sharing, so now is not the time to hesitate. If you look at the really successful and innovative companies and organizations around the world today, they are often the ones that celebrate individual and creative contributions. In a spirit like that, presenting your work and your great ideas is no time to be timid. Life is too short. If you want to change things—including the arc of your own career—then how you present yourself and your ideas matters a great deal. Why not be different?

Seven Lessons from the Bath

The *ofuro* (お風呂), or Japanese bath, is
an integral part of Japanese life. Just as
the meaning of Japanese cuisine goes far
beyond sustenance, the significance of
the bath goes far beyond merely washing.
For generations the *sentō* (銭湯), or "bath
house," was a focal point in residential
areas and a gathering place not just for
bathing but for chatting, meeting friends,
and generally feeling connected to others in the neighborhood. Today there are
fewer sentō as all modern homes have a
private bath, but the significance of the
bathing ritual—whether at home, visiting an onsen, or at the local sentō—runs
deep in the Japanese approach to life,
which traditionally is closely tied to
nature.

A natural hot spring in Japan.

So what can be learned from the Japanese bath as it relates to communication
and presentation? How is a Japanese
bath like a presentation? Here are just
seven ways:

1. You must first prepare.
One must take time to thoroughly wash *before* taking a bath. And one
must fully prepare *before* taking the podium.

2. You must go fully naked.
Shorts and swimming suits are not allowed. You must enter the washing area of an onsen or sentō fully nude (save for a small washcloth).
Presenting naked is about removing the unnecessary to expose what
is most important. Naked presenters do not try to hide but instead
stand front and center and share their ideas in a way that connects
with and engages the audience.

3. Barriers and masks are removed.

Removing our clothes is symbolically removing the façade and the walls that separate us. In today's presentations, visuals are sometimes used as a crutch rather than an amplifier of our message, thus becoming a distraction and a barrier themselves. Visuals in a naked presentation never obfuscate but instead illuminate and clarify. The naked presenter designs visuals that are simple with clear design priorities that contain elements that guide the viewer's eye.

4. You are now fully exposed.

The best type of bathing is in the *roten-buro*, or the outside onsen, especially in fall or winter. The water is hot and the air may be cold, yet you feel alive. Presenting naked is about being free from worry and self-doubt. Gimmicks and tricks and deception are inconsistent with the naked style. You are now transparent, a bit vulnerable, but confident and in the moment.

5. You are on the same level as others.

Hierarchy and status are not apparent or important when naked. The best presentations are less like a lecture. They feel more like an engaging conversation in a language that is clear, honest, and open. Don't try to impress. Instead, try to share, help, inspire, teach, inform, guide, persuade, motivate, or make your audience a little bit better. No matter who you are, a presentation is a chance to make a contribution with fellow humans.

6. You must be careful of the time. Moderation is key.

Nothing is better than soaking in the hot water, but do not overdo it. Too much of a good thing can turn unhealthy. A good presenter also is mindful of time and aware that it is not his or her time but *their* time. Remember the concept of *hara hachi bu*, which means "Eat until 80% full." Give the audience greater quality than expected, but be respectful of their time, and never go over your allotted time. Leave the audience satisfied but not satiated (that is, overwhelmed).

7. Feels great after you're done.

The bath will recharge you as it warms your body and energizes your soul. After an important talk, if it goes well, you also feel invigorated and inspired. If you connect with an audience in a meaningful and passionate way that leaves them with something of value—knowledge, insight, inspiration, even a bit of yourself—then you feel a sense of joy that comes from making an honest contribution.

Going naked and going natural are the key takeaways from the Japanese bath that, with a little creativity, you can apply to many aspects of your work and daily life. In this time of ubiquitous digital presentation and other media tools, the tenets of nakedness and naturalness are more important than ever. At the end of the day, it still remains people connecting and forming relationships with other people. And that's best done naked.

Before you enter the water, you first must *prepare* by
bathing outside the ofuro.

The cold air and the snow are a beautiful and refreshing
contrast to the hot spring water.

About This Book

Even if you have never had a presentation-skills class, the fundamentals of effective delivery are inside you. In this book I simply remind you of some of the principles that you know are important—but nonetheless you may be omitting from your presentations.

As a proponent of design thinking, I embrace constraints. Self-imposed constraints can lead to better focus and more creativity. In writing this book, I decided to limit the core presentation-delivery principles to those that begin with the letter P. I have also limited the number to 10 (plus one extra). There are more than just 10 things that go into developing engaging delivery skills—there are even many more that begin with the letter P—but these 10 in this book will form the basic and hopefully memorable framework for discussing how to greatly improve your ability to connect, engage, sustain, and finish a presentation on a winning note. The "10 Ps" are: Preparation, Punch, Presence, Projection, Passion, Proximity, Play, Pace, Participation, and Power. The extra P is Persistence, a necessary quality to apply in your lifelong commitment to learn and grow as a presenter, a topic touched on in the last chapter.

I believe that many communication, design, and life lessons exist in the artistic disciplines that surround us, though they often go unnoticed. In my case it would be my lifelong study of the art of jazz as well as my study of many of the Zen arts here in my adopted home country of Japan. Along the way, this book periodically introduces lessons from these artistic influences to add a different perspective to the principles.

In Sum

• No matter how much you train, or how extensively you use digital tools in a live presentation, the tools and techniques must be used only to clarify, simplify, and support the personal connection that can develop between an audience and a speaker.

• Natural delivery is more like a conversation between friends or coworkers than a formal, one-way, didactic lecture.

• The potential of your speech or your presentation to change things—maybe even change the world—goes far beyond just the words spoken. An effective presentation allows you to amplify the meaning of your words.

• Presenting your work and your great ideas is no time to be timid. Life is too short. If you want to change things—including the arc of your own career—then how you present yourself and your ideas matters a great deal.

We don't know where we get our ideas from. We do know that we do not get them from our laptops.

— John Cleese

2

First Things First: Preparation

Effective presentations are the result of proper preparation. Ineffective presentations have their genesis in poor planning or in the misguided idea that one can just fake it. You can't fake it and you can't wing it. Going naked and engaging naturally with an audience does not mean approaching the task in a nonchalant or cavalier fashion. Ironically, without proper preparation of your material, you will not be able to be your natural self. You will be disorganized, uncertain, and anxious in spite of your best efforts to show otherwise in front of your audience. An audience can easily pick up on your lack of preparation and this will harm your ability to connect. You do not have to be perfect in your presentation. We are all imperfect by nature and audiences understand that and can forgive a few minor glitches. However, audiences are not forgiving if they sense you have not properly prepared—or if you have not specifically prepared for them—and instead pull out a canned presentation. This chapter touches on a few things to keep in mind as you prepare your presentation.

You Need Alone Time

Presentation is a creative activity and creativity requires you to take some time away from the myriad distractions in your life. You need to quiet your busy mind so you can focus on what is important and ignore what is not. You need to find time alone to achieve clarity of thought. This is increasingly difficult to do in today's world, but you must do what you can to find a time and a place with no interruptions. This applies not only to preparing presentations, of course, but to all creative endeavors that are part of your work.

At the 2008 Creativity World Forum in Flanders, Belgium, the legendary British comedian, actor, and writer John Cleese spoke on the role of creativity in work. He said that a main problem for many of us today is that we are always in a hurry—our minds are scattered as if juggling many balls in the air. If we are racing around all day with a busy mind, Cleese said, we are not going to have many creative ideas. We must slow down our minds to see the connections. Some evidence shows that insights, for example, are best captured when we slow down, clear the noise, and just sort of noodle on a problem. In David Rock's book *Your Brain at Work* (HarperBusiness, 2009), he says, "Having insights involves hearing subtle signals and allowing loose connections to be made. This requires a quiet mind."

Create a "tortoise enclosure"

One key to being more creative, said Cleese, is to avoid interruption. The question, then, is how to become more creative in a frantic, fast-paced world that is filled with interruptions and that demands us to deal with many tasks at the same time. Cleese's idea is that we must create a "tortoise enclosure," an atmosphere that is safe and free from the threat of interruption. We have to create an oasis in the middle of the chaos most of us live in. We must create clear boundaries of space and of time. Creating the space to avoid interruptions may be difficult at home and at work, but it must be done.

If you have a nice private office at work or a good home office, it's easier. If you do not have one of these luxuries, as Cleese mentioned, you can always find some other kind of oasis such as the park, a coffee shop, the beach, and the like. According to Cleese, when we create this "oasis of boundaries" where we cannot be interrupted, we must give ourselves a clear starting time and a clear finishing time. A boundary of time as well as space is important for exploration and creativity to flourish. Exploration and the freedom to play around with ideas happens when there are clear boundaries from ordinary life.

You need time alone to get your ideas together. This time alone does not always have to be in an office setting.

Multitasking myth

Although our lives are very busy and the Internet and social media create tempting distractions virtually every waking hour, preparing a presentation is not something you do best while performing other tasks. In his best-selling book *Brain Rules* (Pear Press, 2009), Dr. John Medina cites findings from reams of cognitive research that indicate we are not even capable of multitasking in the first place. "We are biologically incapable of processing attention-rich inputs simultaneously."

While some people may feel that they are pretty good at moving from one task to another and back again very quickly with great efficiency—what is commonly called multitasking—from the brain's point of view these are still interruptions. And as Medina points out, research shows that people who are interrupted take 50 percent longer to complete a task and make 50 percent more errors. Trying to prepare creative work such as a presentation while simultaneously engaging in other distractions is a recipe for mediocrity.

Get away from the computer

Turn off the computer and go analog during the initial stage of preparation. One of the greatest sources of interruption obviously is our computers and smart phones. "When you're always online you're always distracted," says Dr. Medina. "So the always online organization is the always unproductive organization." You may eventually use a computer for creating and displaying visuals, or at least to type up notes if you are presenting without multimedia, but I have found that great clarity and a fresh perspective can be achieved by temporarily unplugging yourself from the grid and grabbing pens and paper or a whiteboard to sketch out your ideas. In a world that is always online and always connected, it's helpful to get away from your computer as much as possible. As Cleese said, "We don't know where we get our ideas from. We do know that we do not get them from our laptops."

Identify the Purpose

Here in Japan, I once sat through a series of boring presentations during which each presenter went on and on, listing facts and figures about their respective organizations. I was told that the objective of the presentations was to grow membership by trying to convince the audience to join their organizations. What the presenters failed to grasp is that our interest as listeners was in learning of the *benefits* from *our* point of view. We wanted to hear what's in it for us, not how much you can tell us about yourself. We did not need long monologues about the companies' histories, including finances and organizational charts and such.

The presenters surely thought the purpose of their talks was to provide information and talk about themselves, but they identified the wrong purpose. The real purpose should have been to make us (the audience) feel that we were being listened to and our needs were understood, and to show what was in it for us. The presenters failed that day because before they assembled their data-filled slides, they didn't closely consider the real purpose of the event.

Creating a change

When you present, you are trying to create change in people's minds. Your goal may be to teach them something new, share knowledge that is useful and illuminating, motivate and inspire them, or persuade them to change a behavior. Many talks will have elements of all these things. Whatever your specific goals may be, your aim is always to influence a change in people, in whatever short time you have with them. In this sense, you are selling. In an interview with presentations specialist Cliff Atkinson, marketing guru Seth Godin said this about presentations: "It seems to me that if you're not wasting your time and mine, you're here to get me to change my mind, to do something different. And that, my friend, is selling. If you're not trying to persuade, why are you here?"

If you are focused on your audience as you should be, in the preparation stage you need to identify where your audience is *before* your talk—and then set a goal for where you would like them to be *after* your time with them. Author Jerry Weissman calls this moving people from Point A (where they are before the presentation) to Point B (where they are after your talk). Nancy Duarte of Duarte Design talks about this in terms of "Move from" to "Move to," but the idea is essentially the same, and an extremely simple one. It is so fundamental and straightforward, in fact, that you would think every presenter would understand this. Unfortunately, most presenters prepare their talks only by gathering information and facts; they never frame the purpose of their talks in terms of impacting a change in their audience.

Start with why

In his best-selling book *Start with Why* (Portfolio, 2009), author Simon Sinek says that the leaders and companies that have great influence start with the "why" of what they do. They are able to articulate the "why" to inspire and motivate people to do remarkable things. Most organizations and people can say what they do and even how they do it, but few can say why they do it. To answer why, one must have a clarity of purpose. Starting with what is easier and common, but it is insufficient. "People don't buy what you do, they buy why you do it," says Sinek.

In preparing a presentation, too, the most fundamental question to ask yourself first is "Why?" In my first book on presentation design and delivery, *Presentation Zen* (New Riders, 2008), I say that most ineffective presentations can be prevented if the presenter just answers two important questions before beginning to prepare: (1) What's my point? and (2) Why does it matter?

Most presenters focus only on the "what" (information, data, more information, and more data, just in case) and then spend some time on the "how," which often results in the creation of typical bullet-point-driven PowerPoint slides. Almost no time is spent really thinking about the "why." The "why" is where we should start almost all projects, including presentations. Why does your topic and conclusion matter? Why is it important for the audience (or not)? Thinking deeply about the "why" is not an abstraction—it's fundamental. In life, and in business, we spend all of our energy thinking and talking about the "what" and the "how," all the while bombarding audiences with information and no context.

Asking "why" is really a question about the big picture. And when you have a clear idea about why your idea matters and why it should matter to them, you are better able to articulate the significance of your idea in the whole scheme of things. Audiences need the details and they require evidence—but they also need to see the big picture. Articulating the "why" is at the center of this big picture. Design your content in a way that addresses the "why" from the audience's point of view.

The other question to ask yourself is this: Why was I chosen to speak? Why are people coming to see me? The answers to these questions help you identify the real purpose of your talk and put the emphasis on the audience. Right from the start you can tell people why it matters and then spend time showing evidence of this.

To help you identify your core message and make the meaning and purpose of your talk clear, start with "why?"

Christopher Craft

Christopher Craft is an innovative and award-winning educator in Columbia, South Carolina. He presents around the globe on topics ranging from educational theory to cutting-edge technological innovations. Chris works with companies through his education consulting firm called Palmetto Learning, LLC.

www.palmettolearning.com

Chris has the noble goal of providing a classroom environment that is both rigorous and also provides interactive Zen. He offers practical tips for fellow teachers.

Advice for Teachers

Presentations have a purpose. These purposes include a speaker who wants to present a new idea, product, or event. Classroom teachers and university professors often present new subject matter through presentations. During one of these presentations, have you ever found yourself listening to a presenter reading slides full of text? It is easy to wish for a better presentation style, but have you ever wondered what really happens in the minds of audience members during poorly designed presentations?

Human beings have a limited working memory. We forget new names and phone numbers; we even forget where we parked the car at the mall. These items made it into our working memory but did not get encoded into our long-term memory. The human long-term memory system is virtually limitless. This is why we remember trivial pieces of information from the past but often forget where we left our keys. The limits of the human cognitive architecture should play a big role in how we design presentations. For example, humans process auditory and visual stimuli through different channels. This means that text, images, and vocal stimuli should be carefully selected.

Consider the working memory system to be a bit like a glass of water. During a presentation, information (water) is poured into the water glass. If too much water is added too quickly, the glass over-flows. When the working memory system is overloaded, audience members reach cognitive overload. When cognitive overload occurs, the working memory system empties and humans revert to previously learned content. This means that if you overload your audience, everything you've just said will be lost.

You can avoid overloading the minds of your audience members by adopting some of these research-backed principles:

• **Words and vocal stimuli should be disparate, not synchronous.** Or, don't read your slides! When you present the exact same information through both channels, you are pouring too much water into the glass too quickly and will certainly cause overload. Remember, your audience can read the words on your slides faster than you can speak them.

• **Use more than just words.** Using a few carefully chosen words with a high-quality image that is related to the text is a wonderful way to accommodate the dual-channel nature of the human mind.

• **Rehearse your presentation multiple times before presenting.** Time invested rehearsing will pay big dividends, helping you avoid unnecessary pauses or confusion as you speak.

• **Give your audience time to process.** This may take the form of some audience interaction, a moment to discuss with a neighbor, or just a pause to let the audience sip the metaphorical water in the cup.

• **Tell a story.** Using stories helps create an association between your content and a story line. This makes your audience more likely to be engaged with you and your content.

• **Avoid the extraneous**—transitions, sound effects, and other "noise."

Remember that cognitive overload is harmful to your presentation's purpose. If we are not vehemently devoted to avoiding cognitive overload, we may end up preventing learning.

Know your audience

When I was working at Apple in Cupertino, California, I received an email forwarded from Steve Jobs's office. The email was from the leader of a user group whose organization had received a presentation from one of Apple's field engineers the day before. The user group leader was not happy with the presentation and decided to let the CEO of the firm know of his displeasure. My job was to investigate the problem and smooth things over with the user group.

According to the leader of the group, the engineer obviously had deep knowledge of what he was talking about. The material, however, was deeply technical and of little interest to the majority of the audience members. While the group was very interested in technology—especially the latest Apple technology—they were mostly interested in how to *use* the tools and how they can do useful things to improve their creativity or productivity at work and at home. When I talked to the engineer—a very bright and personable young man—he admitted that he knew the presentation was not going well, but he had no idea how to change his content. He continued with his initial plan and did the best he could. The poor presentation and bitter feelings could have been avoided if the presenter simply had understood his audience before he started to prepare.

The engineer had never spoken to a user group before, and he did not have a clear idea of their expectations or backgrounds. He just went with what he knew. Had he understood the user group members' backgrounds, experiences, and expectations, he acknowledged that he would have prepared completely different material and engaged the group in more discussion and Q&A.

The lesson here is that to clearly understand the purpose of your talk and lay the foundation for preparation, you need to know your audience as best you can. This requires a good deal of empathy and ability to put yourself in their shoes. After you find out as much as you can about their backgrounds and expectations—as well as information about cultural differences and things to avoid—you will be better able to choose what material to include and what to exclude. You'll also have a better idea of how to connect with the specific audience and keep them interested and engaged.

Target the whole person

While each audience is different, people are all very similar in at least one regard: they do not like to be bored. A sure way to bore an audience is to remove your personality completely from the talk and focus only on listing streams of information and presenting reams of facts, data, product features, and so on. People need the big picture. They need context and meaning. But they also need to feel some sort of connection to the person speaking.

Aristotle said that good public speaking can be broken into three parts: (1) appeals to reason, (2) appeals to emotions, and (3) appeals based on the character and personality of the speaker. In a good presentation, therefore, you need logical construction and supporting evidence, you need to impact the audience emotionally, and you need to show your character, sincerity, and credibility naturally. People are logical but they are also emotional. Your presentation must target your audience's need for structure and evidence to support your claims, but you must also tap into their emotions through the use of examples, stories, and visualizations. You must appeal to the natural human desire for novelty, exploration, discovery, and the thrill that comes from learning something new.

Deep or wide?

The problem with many presentations is that people try to say too much in a short amount of time. Most people struggle with practicing restraint in the preparation stage, and they have a hard time making the tough choices about what to include before the presentation. Often, no time is given to paring down. As a result, audiences all too often get more than they want, need, or can comprehend. We know this is true of many executive presentations, sales presentations, and conference presentations. In *The Craft of Scientific Presentations* (Springer, 2002), Michael Alley touches on a similar idea and suggests that you can go deep (in depth) or you can go wide (in scope), but it is very difficult to do both in a one-hour lecture or conference presentation. The key is to set realistic goals. If you decide that you need to go deep, you have to seriously consider reducing the scope. Sometimes in life, as in presentations, you just have to make a choice about what's important and let go of the rest (at least for the time being).

You cannot include everything in a talk. If you include too much and race through it, you not only lose the audience, but you eliminate any space for interaction and discussion. People need some time and space to see the patterns and process the material.

Relating too much information—and leaving no time for connecting the dots—is one of the most common communication mistakes, says Dr. Medina. "Lots of force feeding, very little digestion." By excluding some material, you can create some empty space, which leaves room for the audience to ask questions and engage with the subject. Creating this space is more naked and natural as it invites the audience in. By making a clear decision in the preparation stage concerning the depth and scope of your talk, you are better able to include the most important elements and remove the nonessential, thereby creating the space for dialogue.

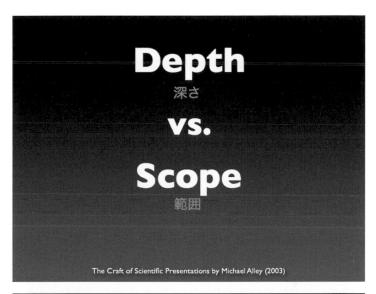

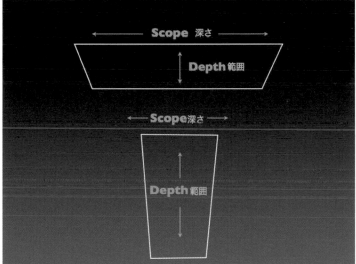

You can go deep or you can go wide but it's very difficult to do both in a single presentation. Slides adapted from *The Craft of Scientific Presentations* by Michael Alley.

When the storytelling goes bad in society, the result is decadence.

— Aristotle

The Power of Story

Story is an important way to engage the audience and appeal to people's need for logic, structure, and emotion. Humans are predisposed to remember experiences in the narrative form; we learn best with a narrative structure. Humans have been sharing information aurally and visually far longer than we have been sharing by reading lists or bulleted points. A 2003 *Harvard Business Review* article on the "power of story," says storytelling is the key to leadership and communication in business. "Forget PowerPoint and statistics, to involve people at the deepest level you need to tell stories."

In an interview with the *Harvard Business Review*, legendary screenwriting coach Robert McKee suggests that a big part of a leader's job is to motivate people to reach certain goals. "To do that she must engage their emotions," McKee says, "and the key to their hearts is story." The most common way to persuade people, says McKee, is with conventional rhetoric and an intellectual process that—in the business world—often consists of typical PowerPoint presentations in which leaders build their case with statistics and data. But people are not moved by statistics alone, nor do they always trust your data. "Statistics are used to tell lies...while accounting reports are often BS in a ball gown."

McKee says rhetoric is problematic because while we make our case, others argue with us in their heads, using their own statistics and sources. Even if you do persuade through argument, says McKee, it's not good enough because "people are not inspired to act on reason alone." The key is to unite an idea with an emotion, which is best done through story. "In a story, you not only weave a lot of information into the telling but you also arouse your listener's emotion and energy," McKee says.

Look for the conflict

A good story is not the beginning-to-end tale about how results meet expectations, McKee says. This is boring. Avoid this. Instead, it's better to illustrate the "struggle between expectation and reality in all its nastiness." What makes life interesting is "the dark side." The struggle to overcome negative powers is what forces us to live more deeply, says McKee. Overcoming negatives is interesting, engaging, and memorable. Stories like this are more convincing.

The biggest element of a story, therefore, is conflict. Conflict is dramatic. At its core, a story is about a conflict between expectations and cold reality. A story is about an imbalance, opposing forces, or a problem that must be worked out. A good storyteller describes what it's like to deal with these opposing forces, such as the difficulty of working with scarce resources; making difficult decisions; or completing a long journey of scientific discovery, trial and error, and so on.

People often prefer to present only the rosy (and potentially boring) picture. "But as a storyteller, you want to position the problems in the foreground and then show how you've overcome them." If you tell the story of how you struggled with the antagonists, says McKee, the audience is engaged with you and your material.

Contrasts are compelling

Whether in graphic design or the components of story, contrast is one of the most fundamental and important elements to include. Contrast is about differences—and we are hard wired to notice differences. You can see contrast everywhere in good storytelling, including film-making. For example, in *Star Wars IV,* there is compelling contrast between the good and noble Rebel Alliance and the dark side of the Death Star and the evil empire. Yet great contrasts also exist between the main characters who are on the same side. The young, naïve, idealistic Luke Skywalker character contrasts with the old, wise, and realistic Obi-Wan Kenobi. The level-headed, diplomatic, and young Princess Leia contrasts with the slightly cocky, irreverent, and older Han Solo. Even R2D2 and C3PO are engaging characters due in large part to their strikingly different personalities. These characters are so compelling to millions of fans because of their inherent contrasts and the series of negotiations they go through as they deal with their differences.

In your own presentations, look for contrasts such as before/after, past/future, now/then, problem/solution, strife/peace, growth/decline, pessimism/optimism, and so on. Highlighting the contrasts is a natural way to bring the audience into your story and make your message more memorable.

These slides show very simple forms of visual contrast: size, texture, shape, color, direction/orientation, age, and so on.

Using storytelling principles in presentations

You do not always have a lot of time to prepare a presentation and sometimes it's difficult to see what the story is. Here are three simple steps you can use to prepare virtually any presentation relatively quickly.

1. **Identify the problem.** For example, this could be a problem that your product solves.
2. **Identify causes of the problem.** Give actual examples of the conflict surrounding the problem.
3. **Show how and why you solved the problem.** This is where you provide resolution to the conflict.

Basically, that's it. Introduce the problem you have (or did have), and how you will solve it (or did solve it). Give examples that are meaningful and relevant to your audience. Remember, story is sequential: "This happened, and then this happened, and therefore this happened, and so on." Take people on a journey that introduces conflict and then resolves that conflict.

If you can do this you will be miles ahead of other presenters, most of whom simply recall talking points and broadcast lists of information. Remember, we tend to forget lists and bullet points, but stories come naturally to us. Stories are how we've always attempted to understand and remember the bits and pieces of our experiences. McKee's point is that you should not fight your natural inclination to frame experiences into a story. You should, instead, embrace this and tell the story of your experience/topic to your audience.

Stories and emotions

Our brains tend to recall experiences and stories that have a strong emotional element to them. The emotional components of stories help them to be remembered. I saw this earlier this year when four students in my Japanese Labor Management class did a presentation on employment security in Japan. Three days later, when I asked other students to recall the most salient points of the presentation, what they remembered most vividly was not the labor laws, the principles, and changes in the labor market in Japan. Rather, they remembered the topic of *karoshi* (literally, "death by overwork") and the issue of suicides in Japan—topics that were quite minor points in the hour-long presentation. About five minutes of the hour-long presentation was spent on karoshi, but that's what the audience remembered most. It's easy to understand why. The issue of death-from-overwork and the relatively high number of suicides are extremely emotional topics that are not often discussed. The presenters cited actual cases and told stories of people who died as a result of karoshi. The stories and the emotional connections they triggered—surprise, sympathy, and empathy—with the audience caused these relatively small points to be remembered most in people's minds.

Telling stories is the natural way humans share information. The stories that get remembered best trigger one or more emotions.

Stories Get Your Attention and Make It Real

This January, we drove Maui's Road to Hana—one of the most beautiful places in the world—to the 'Ohe'o Gulch Falls at Haleakala National Park in Kipahulu. The falls look inviting and are usually calm. But to warn the tourists of the great dangers that lurk, large warnings signs have been installed to advise people to use great caution. Of course, people often ignore warning signs like this. They think the dangers are abstractions that happen to other people, if they happen at all. What I found very effective was that the park service included newspaper clippings of actual accidents that had occurred there recently. I know it was effective because people read

The sign above features newspaper clippings, which underscore the dangers by making this content more emotional, real, and memorable.

these articles and you could see the look of concern on their faces. I usually would only glance at such signs, but I stayed there and read every word. I felt sad for the victims, who were no longer abstractions but real people with names and hometowns; they were mothers, sons, and so on. Reading the accounts of what could happen—what did happen—stopped me in my tracks. It was informative but also emotional. In this case, the elements of information and emotion together made quite an impact and the content was memorable.

A Simplified Process

No successful presentation was ever created by going straight to slideware, typing in content, and following a prepackaged template. Several methods exist for planning a presentation. The following eight steps provide a basic outline of the process I use (a few of which were covered earlier in this chapter). Many successful presenters follow a process that is similar in nature.

1. **Create an oasis of solitude.** Find some space and time to be alone without the possibility of interruption. You need both a place and a set amount of time to quiet your busy mind, see things clearly, and link associations that you may have missed before.
2. **Remove the distractions.** Turn off your computer and unplug yourself from the grid. You'll be amazed at your creativity and insights when you remove the sources of interruptions.
3. **Go analog.** Grab a sketch book, sticky notes, or index cards. Alternatively, place yourself in front of a large whiteboard. You do not need a computer—that comes later (if ever).

College students prepare their presentation together by turning off the computer and sketching their ideas.

4. **Identify your core point.** You know your topic well, have learned about the audience, and thought about what's in it for them. Now you need to identify your core point. Your core point is not the topic. The topic may be something like "report on results of Q4" whereas your core point is "there is great reason to be optimistic because future sales for Q4 exceeded expectations for the first time in three years."

   The core point is that one thing you want people to remember more than anything else. If they remember only one thing, what should it be? So ask yourself, "Is the core point clear in my mind?" Write it down. The key question to answer is where do you want to take your audience? How do you want them to be different or think differently after you are done? Remember: You are always trying to move people from their current place to a new place. The new place is related directly to your core point. What is the core salient point that will have the biggest impact and create a change? In the example here, the audience was skeptical and pessimistic about the future before the talk. They have moved to a state of being more optimistic after the presentation.

5. **Brainstorm.** Generate as many ideas as possible regarding your topic and core point. You need not show restraint here. Editing comes later. In brainstorming, quantity matters. Write your ideas down on cards or sticky notes and place them on a table or whiteboard. This is something you can do by yourself or in a group (if the presentation is a team project). When working in a group, do not judge others' ideas. Simply write down the ideas and place them with the others for the time being. At this stage, even crazy ideas are OK because the offbeat ideas may lead to more practical yet still compelling supporting ideas later on.

6. **Consolidate, edit, and group your ideas.** Now the editing
    begins. This is where you need to show restraint and not try to
    include too much in your talk. Edit ruthlessly. Ideally you want
    to group your ideas into three or four clear categories that can
    be used to support your theme and core point. Remove all the
    points that do not fit into one of these categories.

    The classic storytelling structure is three acts. I have found
    that organizing presentations around three sections that all get
    back to supporting the core point— while taking people on a
    journey of discovery and conflict/resolution—is a good number
    to work with. Structuring a presentation around a single theme
    and a core point with three separate sections that go deeper
    in supporting the core point in different ways is a classic and
    effective organizational technique. (This technique works well
    for speeches, too.) After you have the structure set, go back
    again and see if there is anything you can add or remove to
    increase clarity. Remember, though, that most presentations try
    to include too much—not too little. To present naked means to
    exclude the nonessential. The editing process is mostly about
    subtraction, not addition.

7. **Sketch your visuals.** Now that you have identified a clear theme, a core takeaway message, and two or three sections containing the appropriate amount of detail (including data, stories, quotes, facts, and so on), you can begin to think about visuals. How can you visualize your ideas to make them more memorable and accessible to your audience? Using a sketchbook and sticky notes, or even scratch paper, begin to change the words on your paper or sticky notes into rough sketches of images—images that eventually will become high-quality photography, quantitative displays, charts, slides featuring quotations, and so on.

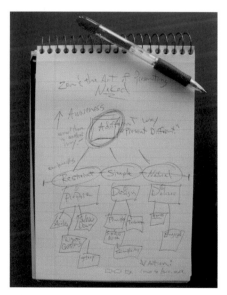

A first-draft rough sketch of the outline with a theme broken into three sections.

8. **Build visuals in software.** Once your structure is complete and you have sketched out the visuals, you can change many of your words into images. Take those sketches and rough visualizations, and build compelling visuals in one of the many popular presentation-software programs. Remember to show great restraint by ignoring most of the software features and instead focusing on creating visuals that are simple, clear, and engaging. Use stock image web sites to find appropriate photos or video clips, or hire a professional photographer if the project requires higher-quality photography (and the budget allows for it). You will find, however, that many images or videos you identify in your sketches can be snapped yourself. The advantage of taking photos and video yourself is that the visuals can be more personal and specific to your messages—plus, there is no chance that the images have been seen before.

After sketching the outline and many of the visuals on paper, you can begin to create structure in software.

What about using notes?

You should not read, or even try to memorize, a speech or presentation. But it is OK to have a single page of easy-to-see notes—especially for a speech—that remind you of the key points. You already know your messages and the structure, so you only need short lines of text or sketches on the paper to remind you of what you already know well. After all, why would you need lengthy notes unless you do not know what you are talking about?

Through your careful preparation you already know the material. There should be no need for copious notes aside from a single page with key points in large type (if you even need that). Although most people do not need notes for a presentation given with multimedia—constantly referring to notes would be a barrier and a distraction—it is a good idea to prepare a one-page list of key points in the unlikely event that your technology dies.

How much should you rehearse?

Each person is different, but you probably need to rehearse a presentation all the way through at least four or five times, or until you feel comfortable. Remember your goal is *not* to memorize the content word for word. By the time you put so much work into preparing, you may only need to go through the entire presentation a few times.

When you rehearse, do not just sit at your computer and mouth the words or run the ideas by in your head as you go through your visuals. Instead, try to simulate the actual presentation as much as possible. Be certain to stand up and speak out loud in the same voice you plan to use the day of your talk. The difference between your first time and second time is huge. This is why it's so important to have a full run-through as if it were live. After you finish the first time, immediately go back and fix or eliminate the bits that did not work.

Use a remote control (for the slides) just as you will in the live presentation. Get comfortable keeping your eyes forward on the audience, only glancing at the monitor or PC in passing to keep you in the sequential flow of the presentation. You should almost never turn around to look at the screen, so practice getting comfortable with this. In working with college students, their most common delivery mistake is spending most of their time looking at and speaking in the direction of the screen. I continually remind students that the same information on the screen is also on the laptop in front of them. Unless you are physically pointing to something on the screen—which you may want to do from time to time—do not turn your body or bend your neck to look at the screen behind you. The delivery of most presentations would be improved if only this simple rule were followed.

David Rock presenting at TEDxTokyo. With the monitor in front, the presenter never needs to turn his back on the audience. (Photo: Patrick Newell.)

The more you rehearse, the more the fear of the unknown is removed. The more the fear is removed, the more confident you will become. As you become more confident, you will feel more relaxed and your confidence will shine through. The thing about confidence is that it's impossible to fake. With practice, you will indeed become a confident speaker. However, it is possible to rehearse too much. You want it to sound natural and fresh, not mechanical or memorized. If you over-rehearse or try to memorize a script, you will diminish your ability to connect and engage the audience in a natural way.

The Day of the Presentation

On the day of your talk, there are three things you can do before you speak that can help you present naked and engage: (1) Arrive early so you can set up the room the way you like and have time to deal with any glitches that may pop up (whether you use multimedia or not), (2) encourage people to sit in the front, and (3) mingle with the audience before you begin your presentation.

Arrive early, prepare the room

It's always important to arrive early, especially if you will be using technology. Set up your computer right away, make sure the audio and projector are working, and confirm that your remote is working well in the room. When using a projector, many people like to turn the lights low (even in smaller venues). But unless you're presenting in a large, ballroom-style room, leave as many lights on as possible. The speaker cannot be in the dark, no matter how good that makes the slides look.

If you are allowed to adjust the room physically, then give yourself plenty of time to do this. Arrange the room to create the most intimate setting possible, given the restraints of the speaking location. Get people close and remove any physical barriers. If there is a lectern in the middle of the stage, ask that it be removed or put to the side. Sometimes the lectern is fixed, so it's not possible to move it, or it's a major hassle for speakers who come after you and still prefer to stand behind the lectern. That's OK—even if the lectern stays in the center of the stage, there is no reason for you to stand behind it.

Encourage people to sit near the front

Years ago I presented to a group of 200 people. That's a good turn-out, but the problem was the hall seated 450. As people arrived, they naturally spread themselves out all over the hall. The presentation went OK, but the overall vibe and sense of connection was definitely lacking compared to earlier talks with similar material. The intimacy was missing.

The next time I faced a similar situation, I asked the audience members to move closer to the front before I began. This instantly created a more lively atmosphere as people began to unconsciously feed off one another's reactions to the presenter (me) on stage. More questions, more discussion, stronger laughter, and more over-all engagement ensued, with me and with each other. That kind of engagement is not possible when audience members sit very far away from each other. Remember: We want the audience close to us, but we want the audience members to be close to each other as well. Whenever possible, block off a section in the back or ask people to come to the front. The excitement, laughter at the funny bits, and the overall connection and participation goes way up when you take a relatively small number of people in a large room and bring them closer to you.

Mingle with the crowd before you start

A mistake novice presenters make is keeping their distance from the audience while people are waiting for the presentation to begin. This is a wasted opportunity. One reason to arrive early is so that you can take care of all of the technical matters and room arrangements before people start showing up. This gives you the peace of mind you need to begin meeting people as they start arriving. You can't meet everyone, obviously. But even if you meet a handful of people and have a couple of conversations with the audience members, you have demonstrated that you are relaxed, happy to be there, and focused on the audience and their needs.

As you meet people and hear their stories, this may give you further insights into their pain and their specific challenges—ideas that you can elaborate on further in your talk. You'll also discover that you may be able to work your conversations into your talk later. For example, let's say you spoke to a well-known businessman named Nathan Bryan before your talk began. During your presentation, then, you may preface one of your key points with "As I was telling Nathan Byran in the audience a few moments ago, the main problem with the strong yen is…"

Another benefit of going into the audience before you start speaking is that you will begin to feel more comfortable and confident as the audience shifts from an abstraction in your mind to a more concrete and unique group of people that you came to converse with. There is nothing to be scared of or worried about. Since your presentation already began (in a sense) 30 minutes earlier while mingling with the crowd, you'll feel much more relaxed and prepared than if you just wait in the wings until your name is called. It will feel more like the continuation of a conversation you already started with the audience than a sudden and scary beginning.

In Sum

• A boundary of time as well as space is important for exploration and creativity to flourish. Quiet your busy mind so that you can focus on what is important and what is not when preparing your presentation.

• Identify your purpose and understand who your audience is. If we focus on our audiences as we should, then in the preparation stage we will identify where our audience is *before* our talk and set a goal for where we would like them to be *after* our time with them.

• When planning your presentation, think of it as a good story that has conflict, contrasts, problems, and solutions. Emotional elements often leave lasting impressions on the audience. Remember to (1) identify the problem, (2) identify causes of the problem, and (3) show how and why you solved the problem.

• On the day of the presentation: (1) Arrive early so you can set up the room the way you like and have time to deal with any technical glitches, (2) encourage people to sit in the front, and (3) mingle with the audience before you begin your presentation.

The most precious gift we can offer others is our presence.

— Thich Nhat Hanh

3

Connect with Punch, Presence, and Projection

This year I attended a business presentation in Tokyo that taught an important lesson on ineffectiveness. For example, while the host was reading a long introduction of the speaker, everyone was focused on the speaker's computer booting up on the large screen in the center of the room. The screen soon displayed a window asking for the presenter's password. After the applause died down and the lights were dimmed, the speaker was still trying to remember the correct password. "Just a moment," he said as he found the password in his wallet. After he finally got PowerPoint working, and we all enjoyed viewing his desktop with pictures of his children, he spent the next hour in the darkened corner behind a lectern paraphrasing each of the many bullet points that filled the screen—a screen positioned in the center of the room far from the speaker. He looked down at his notes about half the time and looked at the screen across the room for most of the other half. The speaker covered lots of material, but made absolutely no connection with the audience. In spite of the polite applause, the presentation was a waste of time for everyone concerned. It's memorable today only for the boredom it caused—not for the minds that it changed. Content alone is never sufficient. We need an emotional connection with the audience to have an impact. This chapter offers three simple thoughts on how to establish connections with audiences—Punch, Presence, and Projection—the three Ps.

Begin with Punch

During a recent lunch with a CNN news anchor who was visiting Japan, I asked him if he had any presentation advice for novice speakers. Since he makes hundreds of presentations on and off camera every year, I was keen to hear what he had to say about what comprises a successful presentation. Without any hesitation he threw his clenched fist in the air and said in a loud voice, "You've got to reach right out immediately and grab them...and squeeze!" The beginning is the most important part. You need an opening that is punchy. If you fail to hook them at the start, he said, the rest of your presentation may be for naught.

It's so important that you begin with a punchy opening that I highly recommend you ditch the normal opening lines, which go something like this: "Ladies and gentlemen of the association and honored guests, it's genuinely a privilege to be here today in front of all of you at this respected and beloved institution speaking before such a distinguished audience. Thankfully the weather is fabulous today, which is a welcome change from the awful winter we experienced, and furthermore, blah, blah, blah." Resist the long, drawn-out formalities. A simple "thank you" or "good morning" and a smile is fine, and then get right to it.

Make an impact with P.U.N.C.H.

According to the "primacy effect," as applied to presentations, we best remember what happens at the beginning of a presentation more than any other part. To establish a connection with an audience, we must grab their attention right from the beginning. A punchy opening that gets the audience's attention is paramount. Granville N. Toogood, author of *The Articulate Executive* (McGraw-Hill, 1996) also stresses the idea of starting off quickly and beginning with punch. "To make sure you don't get off on the wrong foot, plunge right in," he says. "To galvanize the mind of the audience, you've got to strike quickly."

There are many ways to strike quickly, start with punch, and make a strong initial connection. Conveniently, at least five proven ways to begin a talk form the acronym PUNCH: Personal, Unexpected, Novel, Challenging, or Humorous. The best presentations usually contain at least one or more of these elements. (Included here are the slides that serve as a backdrop when I speak to audiences about PUNCH.)

Personal

Make it personal. I once saw an amazing presentation on workplace safety at a company whose employees have dangerous jobs. The presenter started off his presentation with a high-resolution image of some cute children. After talking about how important our children are (most people in the audience had children), he confessed that the children on screen were his and that his main concern in his life was being around a long while to take care of them. We all have a responsibility, he said, to our families and to each other to make sure we pay careful attention to safety procedures and rules so that nobody's children ever have to be told that mommy or daddy is not coming home. This opening was emotional, personal, and relevant. It got everyone's attention and set the stage for the presentation. What could have been a presentation that simply listed safety rules in bullet points became something far more personal.

There are many ways to make the opening personal, but personal does not mean a long self-introduction about your background complete with organizational charts or why you are qualified to speak. A personal story, however, can be a very effective opening as long as it illustrates a key engaging point or sets the theme in a memorable way.

Unexpected

Reveal something unexpected. Doing something or saying something that goes against what people expect gets their attention. Even the very fact that you have chosen to eschew the normal and expected formal opening of thanking everyone under the sun and saying how happy you are to be speaking is a happy and small  surprise. Instead of the typical formal, slow opening, consider opening with a shocking quote, a question with a surprising answer, or a revealing statistic that goes against conventional wisdom. Do or say something that taps into the emotion of surprise. This emotion increases alertness and gets people to focus. "There must be surprise...some key facts that are not commonly known or are counterintuitive," says management guru Tom Peters. "No reason to do the presentation in the first place if there are no surprises."

Novel

Show or tell something novel. Start with a powerful image that's never been seen, reveal a relevant short story that's never been heard, or show a statistic from a brand-new study that gives new insights into a problem. Chances are that your

audience is filled with natural-born explorers who crave discovery and are attracted to the new and unknown. Novelty is threatening for some people, but assuming the environment is safe and there is not an overabundance of novelty already in the environment, your audience will respond positively to something new.

Challenging

Challenge conventional wisdom or challenge the audience's assumptions. Consider challenging people's imaginations, too: "How would you like to fly from New York to Tokyo in two hours? Impossible? Well, some experts think it's possible!" Challenge people intellectually by asking provocative questions that make them think. Many

presentations or lectures fail simply because they attempt to transfer information from speaker to listener as if the listeners were not active participants. But audiences pay attention best when you call on them to use their brains—and even bodies—to do something that taps their natural curiosity and expand their minds.

Humorous

Use humor to engage the audience emotionally with a shared laugh. There are many benefits to laughter. Laugher is contagious. An audience that shares a laugh becomes more connected with each other and with you, creating a positive general vibe in the room. Laughter releases endorphins, relaxes the whole body, and can even change

one's perspective just a bit. The old adage is if they are laughing they are listening. While this is true, it does not necessarily mean they are learning. It is critical that the humor be directly relevant to the topic at hand or otherwise fit harmoniously with the flow of your narrative without being distracting or derailing you from the objective of your talk.

Using humor in a presentation gets a bad rap because of the common and tired practice of starting a speech with a joke, almost always a lame one. Usually such jokes get only polite sympathy laughter at best, and at worst the joke falls completely flat or even offends. Either way the presenter is off to a poor start. But I'm not talking about telling jokes. Forget about jokes. An observation of irony, an anecdote, or a short humorous story that makes a relevant point, introduces the topic, or sets the theme, on the other hand, is the kind of opening that can work.

There are many ways to start a presentation, but however you choose to start your talk, do not waste those initial valuable two to three minutes "warming up" the audience with filler or formalities. Start strong. The five elements comprising PUNCH are not the only things to consider, but if your opening features two or three of these approaches, then you are on your way to opening with impact.

A presentation is no place to be timid—start with punch and get the audience's attention. (Photo of Phil Waknell presenting in Paris.)

The honeymoon period

Getting and keeping an audience's attention can be a tricky thing. Generally, audiences want you to succeed but will still give you only about one or two minutes of a so-called honeymoon period to make a good impression. Even famous, well-established presenters—including celebrities—will only get about a minute before audiences grow tired of their inability to grab attention.

A couple of years ago I flew from Osaka, Japan, to Stanford University in Palo Alto, California, for a presentation to one of the departments on campus. I was scheduled to arrive that morning with several hours to spare. Due to a late takeoff from Japan and traffic on the freeways, I arrived in the presentation room with briefcase and computer in hand—literally one minute before the scheduled start time—to find a room full of people already sitting down and ready for the presentation to begin. All eyes were now on me. (Gulp.) If I started to set up right away, it would take me several minutes to get everything ready. But fidgeting with technology as you ask for patience is a very weak way to begin and makes a lousy first impression. So, instead, I instantly launched into a conversation with the audience about some of the good and bad presentations they see in their work and how design thinking can play a part in creating better presentations. Then, while they were engaged in a discussion activity I gave them—which created a loud buzz in the room—I quickly connected the computer to the projector and got everything set. In just a few moments, I was ready to continue leading the discussion we had already started. People form impressions of you and the presentation in the first few moments—and you never want those first few moments to be a memory of you trying to get the technology to work.

Be Like Bamboo:
Seven Lessons from the
Japanese Forest

The forests that surround our village here in Nara, Japan, are filled with beautiful bamboo plants. In Japan, the symbolism of the bamboo plant runs deep and wide and offers practical lessons for life and for work. Here, I summarize the lessons with presentation and learning in mind. But as you read these seven lessons, think of practical implications for your own work, including presentations.

1. Bend but don't break. Be flexible yet firmly rooted.
One of the most impressive things about bamboo in the forest is how it sways with even the slightest breeze. This gentle swaying movement is a symbol of humility. Bamboo stems are hard and firm and yet sway gently in the breeze while their trunks stay rooted firmly in the ground below. Their foundation is solid even though bamboo moves harmoniously with the wind, never fighting against it. In time, even the strongest wind tires itself out, but bamboo remains standing. A bend-but-don't-break or go-with-the-natural-flow attitude is one of the secrets for success whether we're talking about bamboo, answering tough questions in a Q&A session, or dealing with the everyday vagaries of life.

2. Remember: What looks weak is strong.

Bamboo is not large by any means when compared to other, much larger trees in the forest. It may not look impressive at first sight at all. But the plants endure cold winters and extremely hot summers and are sometimes the only plants left standing in the aftermath of a typhoon. They may not reach the heights of the other trees, but they are strong and stand tall in extreme weather. Bamboo is not as fragile as it may appear, not by a long shot. Remember the words of a great Jedi Master: "Size matters not. Look at me. Judge me by my size do you?" We must be careful not to underestimate others or ourselves based only on notions of what is weak and what is strong. You may not be from the biggest company or a graduate of the most famous school, but like bamboo, stand tall, believe in your own strengths, and know that you are as strong as you need to be.

3. Be always ready.

Unlike other types of wood, which take a good deal of processing and finishing, bamboo needs little of that. As the great aikido master Kensho Furuya says in *Kodo: Ancient Ways*, "The warrior, like bamboo, is ever ready for action." In presentation or other professional activities, through training and practice, you can develop in your way a state of being ever ready.

4. Unleash your power to spring back.

Bamboo is a symbol of good luck and one of the symbols of the New Year celebrations in Japan. The important image of snow-covered bamboo represents the ability to spring back after experiencing adversity. In winter, the heavy snow bends the bamboo back and back until one day the snow becomes too heavy, begins to fall, and the bamboo snaps back up tall again, brushing aside all the snow. The bamboo endured the heavy burden of the snow, but in the end it has the power to spring back as if to say, "I will not be defeated."

5. Find wisdom in emptiness.

In order to learn, it is said that the first step is to empty ourselves of our preconceived notions. One cannot fill a cup that is already full. The hollow insides of bamboo stems reminds us that we are often too full of ourselves and our own conclusions. We have no space for anything else. To receive knowledge and wisdom from both nature and people, we have to be open to that which is new and different. When you empty your mind of your prejudices, pride, and fear, you become open to the possibilities.

6. Commit to (continuous) growth.

Bamboo plants are among the fastest-growing in the world. It does not matter who you are—or where you are today—you have amazing potential for growth. I often speak of *kaizen* (continuous improvement that is more steady and incremental), where big leaps and bounds are not necessary. Yet even with a commitment to continuous learning and improvement, our growth—like the growth of bamboo—can be quite remarkable when we look back at what or where we used to be. Even though the bamboo outside my window grows quite rapidly, I do not notice its growth from day to day. Even when we are making progress, we may not notice our own improvement. How fast or how slow is not our main concern, only that we're moving forward. The bamboo grows fastest around the rainy season. You, too, may have "seasons" during which growth accelerates, and other times when growth is slower. Yet with sustained effort, you are always growing. Do not be discouraged by what you perceive as your lack of growth or improvement. If you have not given up, then you are growing—you just may not see it until much later.

7. Express usefulness through simplicity.

Aikido master Kensho Furuya says, "The bamboo in its simplicity expresses its usefulness. Man should do the same." Indeed, we spend a lot of our time trying to show how smart we are, perhaps to convince others—and ourselves—that we are worthy of their attention and praise. Often we complicate the simple to impress and we fail to simplify the complex out of fear that others may already know what we know. Life and work are complicated enough without our interjecting the superfluous. If we lose our fear, perhaps we can be more creative and find simpler solutions to even complex problems that ultimately provide the greatest usefulness for our audiences, customers, patients, or students.

As a renewable material, bamboo is versatile, elegant, refined, and yet humble. Bamboo offers us many life lessons in its natural simplicity and strength.

Never start with an apology

Do not apologize, imply, or even admit that you have not prepared enough for your specific audience. It may be true, and your apology may be coming from a sincere, honest place (rather than just making an excuse), but it never comes across well to an audience. The audience does not need to know that you feel as if you have not prepared as much as you would have liked, so why mention it and get it in their heads? You actually may be sufficiently prepared and doing well, but now the audience members are saying to themselves, "Man, he's right—he didn't prepare enough."

The same principle goes for telling people you're nervous. "You didn't look nervous, but now that you mention it...." A confession that you are nervous may seem honest and naked, but it is too self-focused at a time when you are supposed to be focused on the audience and their needs and feelings. An admission of being nervous is not said to make the audience feel better, only to make you feel better. If you admit that you are nervous, you may actually feel better since labeling and acknowledging an emotion is better than suppressing it. This is why people say it: Saying it out loud does make you feel a little better. Yet the presentation is about the audience. Telling them how nervous you are does not serve their interest. Acknowledge to yourself that you are nervous—and that it is normal—but do not share this information with the audience.

Do you need to show the structure?

I recommend that you not start with an agenda slide. But, after you have made an initial connection with the audience, it's a good idea to give people an idea where you are going in the time you have with them. You can usually do this verbally, in just a few seconds. If you have a lot of material, however, you may want to show the audience how your talk is structured and then remind them along the way where you are in the presentation. In a 2007 Macworld keynote presentation, Steve Jobs did this by breaking his presentation into three "Acts" and displaying the number of the act before each of the three sections.

Another alternative is to clearly articulate the number of sections and how long each section will generally take as a percentage of the time allotted. The following example is for a one-hour talk I gave that covered a lot of material. This slide gives people an overall sense of where we are going.

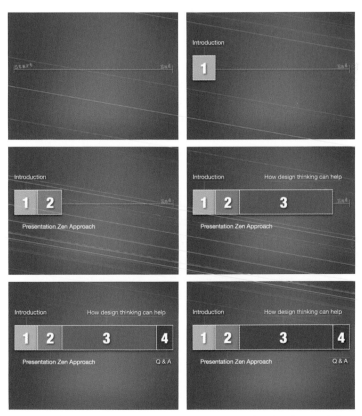

One alternative to bullet points is to introduce your outline visually using a variation of a timeline. Bars and titles wipe from left to right as I introduce the structure.

Establish Presence

Presence is about recognizing the importance of now. It's a frame of mind that says, in effect, there is no past and there is no future. There is only this moment and this presentation and this audience. Being in the moment forces you to slow down and rid yourself of worries about the past and future. Think of how you feel when you meet someone new and have a good conversation that you wish could continue longer. Compare that to how you feel after having a conversation you wish you'd never started and could not wait to escape from. One cause of a poor conversation is a person who goes through the formality, and may even say the right things, but all the while seems to be someplace else and only superficially interested in you. We know when someone is holding back, is uncomfortable, or seems to have other thoughts on their mind. Just like a good conversationalist, a presenter with good presence will connect with you on some level and demonstrate with sincerity that, at least for the moment, he or she does not wish to be anywhere else than right there having a dialogue with you.

Focus on the here and now

We are all so busy running around from meeting to meeting and from place to place that it's easy to lose focus on any particular presentation or particular audience. When I'm under pressure to organize and then deliver a presentation to a new audience, I repeatedly push myself to focus only on this presentation and this audience even though there are a lot of other responsibilities I must deal with that are attempting to interrupt my focus. "This is the presentation," I say to myself. "There are no other presentations." I say this to myself before I begin speaking to a new audience, regardless if it's an audience of 50 or 5,000. For more than 20 years I've used a technique inspired by the 1982 Oscar-nominated film *The Verdict* starring Paul Newman. In this film, Newman plays a struggling, down-on-his-luck lawyer who, facing impossible odds, repeats to himself the mantra "This is the case, there are no other cases." The mantra gets him to focus on the urgency of now—not his past successes and not his recent and numerous failures—as he fights to prepare and ultimately deliver his case. Even if you are not a trial lawyer, there is an important lesson here for professionals of all kinds, and it is simply this: Do not dwell on the past or worry about the future. There is only this case, that is, there is only this presentation. Your audience requires your full focus and attention, just as you ask for theirs, and they will easily notice if you are not fully present in the moment.

Take a risk and express your true self

When you dwell on techniques for winning over someone, worry about what others may think, or fret over whether or not you said the right thing, your mind is not in the present. You are not free. You're in the future or you're in the past, but you are not there with your audience. Sometimes, you just have to take a risk and be your natural self. Amazing connections happen when you take a chance and throw yourself into your presentation without concern for failure or success. Your only concern should be making a contribution and engaging in an honest conversation the best you can in that moment. When you unburden your mind from fear and doubt, your natural self comes out and you'll achieve greater focus and clarity, which creates stronger connections with the audience. Ask yourself this: If you could remove all the fear, what would you do differently? If you remove the doubt concerning the outcome of your presentation, how would you prepare and deliver in a way that is truer to your natural self?

Job interviews are a kind of presentation as well. Several years ago I had my best job interview ever because I was able to remove the fear completely. In fact, I did not have one worry at all about being offered the job, something that usually weighs on an applicant's mind and interferes with his or her ability to be completely natural.

But in this case I had received a job offer from another company the day before—an offer I planned to accept. Yet, because I was still interested in finding out more about the other job, I kept my appointment. When I arrived at the interview, three very serious-looking and rather stiff businesspeople sat on the opposite side of the table and began asking many international business and hypothetical strategy questions.

Normally, this type of interview—which felt a little like an interrogation—might make me at least a little nervous. But because I had removed all worry about the outcome of our hour-long interview, I was able to totally relax and I actually rather enjoyed sharing my ideas and asking questions of my own. A level of passion, spontaneity, and naturalness came over me that I had only experienced before when having impassioned conversations with good friends. By the latter half of the interview, the three people on the other side of the table were smiling, leaning slightly forward across the table, and going off script as our conversation developed.

By focusing on being in the moment and not worrying about outcomes, you can be your natural self even in tough job interviews.

I did not realize it until after the interview, but what I experienced was the kind of freedom, naturalness, and connection in communication that results when you are able to completely focus only on the content and your audience without self-doubt or worry about the future outcome. Since that day I have tried to apply the same focus to all presentations as well. Outcomes do matter. But during the actual presentation, all concern and focus must be in that moment with that particular audience. When you remove the worry about outcomes, you are able to be your natural self and audiences will know the difference. Your naturalness will likely be a refreshing change.

The attraction of authenticity

Authenticity is a big component of presence and people are absolutely attracted to authenticity. Audiences do not need perfection and they certainly do not want someone slick, polished, and over-rehearsed rattling off talking points. Audiences yearn to listen to real people who are honest, sincere, and naked. Commenting on the power and rarity of authenticity, Mike Rowe—host of the Discovery Channel's "Dirty Jobs" and narrator for many TV shows including "Deadliest Catch"—made a beautiful comment about authenticity in a 2010 article he wrote in memory of the late Captain Phil (Phil Harris), a very popular figure in the show "Deadliest Catch":

> *I guess it comes down to this. The world is desperate for authenticity. In business and in real life. In work and play. We crave it I think, because it's in such short supply. Consequently, when we see it, we'll wait for it. We'll watch it on TV. We'll stand in line for a chance to be near it. Fans, fishermen, CEOs—we know authenticity when we see it, even if we're not looking for it. [Phil Harris] was the real deal. Flawed, human, decent, kind, and totally authentic. And one hell of a captain.*
>
> — *Mike Rowe*

The kind of authenticity that Captain Phil exhibited might seem a million miles away from a book on presentations, but the essence is the same. Captain Phil and his great popularity remind us that we do not need to be perfect to make a meaningful connection. But we do need to be our natural, true, and authentic selves. It comes in many forms and it's impossible to quantify, but audiences always know it when they see it.

Avoid reading a speech

In the early days after the first iPod launch in October 2001, I accompanied one of the product marketing managers at Apple to a local user group meeting where loyal Mac enthusiasts were eager to see and hear more about the new product. If you only listened to her, you would know that the Apple employee knew her material very well and obviously knew everything there was to know about the iPod. However, she was not experienced at presenting in the informal style typical of a user group event. She was a bit stiff and formal in front of the audience, who considered themselves to be part of the team rather than customers to be sold to in formal business language. But the thing that hurt her ability to make a good connection with the audience the most was her reliance on notes. She only looked at her notes a few times, but many user group leaders found this very strange. It suggested, they said, that she did not totally understand what she was talking about. She actually had complete knowledge of the product, but it was amazing how a simple thing like occasionally looking down at notes can inhibit one's ability to connect with certain audiences.

Communications guru Bert Decker urges speakers to avoid reading a speech whenever possible. In his book *You've Got to Be Believed to Be Heard* (St. Martin's Press, 2008), Decker says, "Reading is boring.... Worse, reading a speech makes the speaker look inauthentic and unenthusiastic." This goes for reading slides as well. Many years ago the typical use of slideware involved people actually reading lines of text right from the slides behind them, and believe it or not, it still happens today. But don't do it. Putting lots of text on a slide and then reading that text is a great way to alienate your audience and ruin any hopes you have of making a connection.

Guy Kawasaki, cofounder of Alltop.com and author of *Enchantment: The Art of Changing Hearts, Minds, and Actions* (Portfolio, 2011), urges people to use large type on slides that people can actually see. "This forces you, he says, "to actually know your presentation and just put the core of the text on your slide." This is what the outspoken Kawasaki had to say about the idea of reading text off your slides in a speech he gave to a room full of entrepreneurs in Silicon Valley in 2006:

> *If you need to put 8-point or 10-point fonts up there it's because you do not know your material. If you start reading your material because you do not know your material, the audience is very quickly going to think that you are a bozo. They are going to say to themselves 'This bozo is reading his slides. I can read faster than this bozo can speak. I will just read ahead.'*
>
> *— Guy Kawasaki*

Guy's comments got a lot of laughs, but he's right. If you plan to read PowerPoint slides, you might as well call off the presentation now, because your ability to connect and persuade your audience or teach them anything will approach zero. Reading slides is no way to show presence, make a connection, or even transfer information in a memorable way.

Never read your slides.

Project Yourself

Once I attended a presentation by someone I knew to be very intelligent, confident, and charismatic. He was a dynamic person and fun to be around, so I was sure his presentation would be engaging, entertaining, and remarkable. But it was none of those things. The problem was not his content or his preparation; he was well prepared to speak. The problem was he failed to make any lasting connection with the audience because that confident, charismatic person I knew him to be off the stage was not coming across to the audience who was meeting him for the first time. Although the audience found the speaker to be nice enough and reasonably knowledgeable, he unintentionally and unknowingly projected an image of someone who was weak, indecisive, and unsure of himself. He failed, in other words, to project himself—and thus his message—to the large audience before him.

When evaluating your own ability to project yourself to your audience (aside from the content of the talk), there are three things to consider: the way you look, the way you move, and the way you sound. Your audience, whether they know it or not, is judging you and your message based on these three elements.

Look the part

How you dress matters. Most presentation coaches, as a rule of thumb, advise you to dress at least a little more formally than your audience. It's important to dress appropriately to the organization and the occasion, of course, but it's better to be a bit overdressed than underdressed. You want to project an image of professionalism—although you do not want to seem out of touch with your audience either. In Silicon Valley, for example, the dress code can be quite casual; even a well-groomed person in jeans with a nice quality shirt and good pair of shoes may look professional. In Tokyo, both men and women cannot go wrong with a dark business suit, virtually anywhere.

You can always bring your formality down a notch by removing your jacket, removing the tie, and rolling up the sleeves. It's difficult, however, to dress up a look that is too casual. To be safe, and to show respect for your audience, err on the side of dressing formally and professionally.

Move with purpose

If you can, avoid standing in one place during the entire presentation. It's far better to walk to different parts of the stage or the front of the room, which allows you to engage with more people. However, you should not pace back and forth or wander around the area near the screen without purpose. This kind of movement is distracting and projects a nervous—rather than a confident and open—energy.

When you walk from one area to another, do so slowly while standing tall. Stop to make your point or tell a story, then move again, slowly, to another part of the stage before stopping again to elaborate on a different point. When someone asks a question from the opposite side of the room, walk slowly in their direction, acknowledging their presence, while listening and approaching his or her side of the room. As long as people can still hear you, it is a good idea to walk into the audience from time to time—provided there is a purpose for doing so (such as answering a question during an activity you gave the audience).

When you stand, do so with your feet comfortably but firmly planted about shoulder-width apart. Don't stand like a cowboy about ready to draw his guns or with your legs close together as if standing at attention. Standing at attention or with your legs crossed demonstrates a closed, defensive, or uncertain attitude; these are also unnatural ways to stand when relaxed. In these positions, you are a bit unstable physically and the imbalance is projected as weakness to others. Also be careful not to lean against the lectern. At best it looks sloppy and at worst it projects an image of tiredness.

When we get nervous, most of us tend to speed up our movements, including hand gestures. To project a more calm, relaxed, and natural image, remind yourself to slow everything down.

Face the audience

Even if visuals are projected behind you, there is no need to turn your head to look back except for the very briefest of moments. When you gesture toward the screen, stand so that your shoulders are facing in the direction of the audience. If you keep your shoulders pointed toward the front, you will naturally turn your head back toward the audience after glancing at the screen. Turning slightly and briefly toward the screen to point out a detail is acceptable. However, continually looking at the screen behind you or across the stage from you—simply to remind you what is up on the screen—is distracting and unnecessary behavior. Except in rare incidents, when you use a computer to project visuals you can place the computer down low in front of you so there is little reason to have to turn around.

Connect with eye contact

Related to the importance of facing the audience is establishing good eye contact. Maintaining natural eye contact with the audience is crucial. It's one of the reasons I advise against reading a script or relying on notes—it's hard to look into people's eyes when your own eyes are looking down at notes. Your eye contact should appear natural. To achieve this, look at actual people in the room. (If, instead, you gaze out at the back of the room or to a point on either side of the room, your audience will detect this at some level and the connection will be weakened.) If your audience is relatively small, fewer than 50 or so, it may be possible to actually look everyone in the eye at some point during your talk as you move deliberately to different parts of the stage. For larger audiences in a typical keynote-style presentation, it is still useful to pick out actual people to lock eyes with as you speak—even people who are sitting toward the back. By looking at one person, others nearby will feel you are looking at them as well. Professional singers use this technique when playing larger halls. It is important to not just glance at or scan general areas of a room, but rather to briefly establish actual eye contact with individuals in different parts of the room.

Brand communications expert Jakob Lusensky gives an energetic presentation at TEDxTokyo. Lusensky made natural, engaging eye contact as he moved around the stage. (Photo: Patrick Newell.)

Put energy in your voice

It's true that the best presentations seem more like good conversations. There is a difference, however, between speaking with two or three people over coffee and standing to present to an auditorium of 500 people after lunch. Your tone should be conversational, but your energy must be cranked up several notches. If you are enthusiastic, the energy will help your voice project. Mumbling is absolutely not permitted—but that does not mean that you need to shout. Shouting is usually not sustainable and it's very unpleasant for the audience. When you shout, the volume may go up but the richness of your voice, the peaks and valleys of your own unique intonation, are lost. So stand tall, speak up, articulate clearly, but be careful not to let your speaking evolve into shouting as you project your voice.

Should you use a mic? In a regular-size classroom or conference room with space for only 10 to 30 people, a mic may not be necessary. For almost every other case, a microphone is a good idea. Remember, it is not about you, it is about the audience. Providing even just a slight bump in your volume with the use of a microphone will make it easier for the audience to hear you.

Many presenters eschew a mic and opt to shout instead. Men especially do this, as if declining a microphone and choosing to shout is somehow more manly and assertive. But unless you are a head coach delivering an inspiring halftime speech for your football team, shouting is a very bad idea. You are not addressing your troops; you are trying to present in a natural, conversational manner. Far from being a barrier to connection, the microphone can actually be a great enabler of more intimacy—because it allows you to project in your best and most engaging natural voice.

Use a handheld mic only for very short speeches or announcements. A better option is a wireless lavalier mic, also called a clip-on or lapel mic. The lavalier is good because it frees up a hand, which is especially important if your other hand is holding a remote control. The downside of a lavalier is that when you turn your head to the side, some mics will not pick up your voice as well. The best type of microphone is a headband or headset variety, which are used for conferences such as TED. The tiny tip of the mic sits just to the side of your mouth or your cheek and is virtually invisible to the audience. The advantage of this mic—besides eliminating the possibility of ruffling noises from your shirt—is that no matter how you move your head, it stays in the same position, always picking up your voice clearly. Use a headset mic whenever possible.

Pulitzer Prize-winning photojournalist Renée Byer (top) and famed nutritional strategists Sherry Strong (bottom) are shown here using a wireless headset microphone which provides excellent amplification and keeps their hands free. (Photos: TEDxTokyo, Patrick Newell.)

Leave the lights on

For you to make a connection with an audience, they need to be able to see you. Naked means never hiding in the dark. When the audience can actually see your eye movement and read your facial expressions, they will better understand your message. The audience is interpreting meaning based on the verbal (your actual words), the vocal (your voice), and the visual (your nonverbal language). Your nonverbal signals are a very important part of your message. But if people cannot see you—even if they can see the slides fine—much of the richness of your message will be lost.

While it may be tempting to turn the lights off to make the slides look better, maintaining light on the presenter must be the priority. You can often work out a compromise by dimming only some of the lights. Given the advances in projection technology, you can usually keep all or most of the lights on in conference rooms and lecture halls today. Auditoriums usually have better lighting setups, which allow for light on the presenter but off the screen. No matter what kind of presentation situation you are in, make sure there is plenty of light on you. You cannot make a connection if they cannot see you.

Gain Confidence

For the majority of people—even professional entertainers—public speaking is a scary thing. Why is this? There are two possibilities. One possibility is that fear, stemming from the limbic system in our brain, is a completely natural emotion that evolved over time. More than anything else, our brains are designed to keep us alive. The limbic system is always doing its best to help us maximize rewards and minimize threats. If we look at it from an evolutionary point of view, surely conditions for survival favored people whose brains were good at recognizing threats and moving them away from those threats— quickly. Now, standing out from a crowd where you could be an easy target for prey, or having all eyes of a large group focused upon you, was surely regarded as a threatening situation—at least as far as the paleomammalian brain was concerned.

On the other hand, most young children are all too happy to stand up in front of others during "show and tell" or other related activities and share their stories. Perhaps the fear most of us have of public speaking is learned over time based on bad experiences—such as being criticized for our ideas or ridiculed for the way we looked as awkward teenagers. These memories stay with us and may grow stronger over time as we associate negative emotions with standing up and standing out. This is surely at the root of the fear of speaking for some people in addition to the evolutionary possibilities.

Whether the fear of standing before others is learned, innate, or a little of both, what we do know is when the "public speaking threat" is detected, the hypothalamus kicks in and signals the adrenal glands to shoot adrenaline through our body. This causes us to feel panic and the urge to escape, otherwise known as the fight or flight response. It's a very unpleasant feeling, but worse than that, when the limbic system is activated to this degree, our ability to use our prefrontal cortex is temporarily reduced and our ability to pay attention, solve problems, and think on our feet suffers.

Managing your fear

While I mentioned before that you should never admit to an audience that you are nervous, being aware of your emotional state and admitting it to yourself can help you regulate the fear. Do not try to suppress the emotion, as this will usually make things worse. In *Your Brain at Work* (HarperBusiness, 2009), David Rock suggests two cognitive strategies for dealing with your fear. One technique is labeling, which is the practice of simply recognizing the emotion by assigning a word to it. This simple behavior is no panacea, but it has been shown to decrease the negative arousal people are experiencing. The other technique to regulate your emotion is reappraisal. When you reappraise the emotion, you reframe it or change your interpretation of it. Rather than letting the emotion overwhelm your ability to perform, once you become aware of the fear you can immediately say something to yourself, such as, "Well, looks like the old fight-or-flight response is kicking in. It's normal and nothing to worry about. Everyone gets it, so I'll just do some deep breathing and stretching to loosen up my body. No big deal!"

Another thing I have found that significantly reduces anxiety is simply being well prepared. The more you are on top of your material, the less nervous you will be. If you took the time to build a logical structure for your presentation, and designed supporting materials that are professional and appropriate, you will have much less to be nervous about. If you have rehearsed with a computer and projector (assuming you are using slideware) several times, your anxiety will become much more manageable. We fear what we do not know. If we know our material well and have rehearsed the flow, know what slide is next in the deck, and have anticipated questions, then we can eliminate much (but not all) of the unknown. When you remove the unknown, you reduce anxiety and confidence will naturally begin to take the place of your anxiety.

Through practice your confidence will grow and you will feel more relaxed, which enables you to be your natural, engaging self. Once you stop the chatter in your head, the self-doubt, your obsession with technique, and the concern over failure or success, then you are able to simply tell your story and engage with the material and audience. It's just a presentation and you cannot do any better than you can do at that moment. You're just human and so are they.

Standing in front of a crowd is naturally scary for everyone. Acknowledging the natural fear helps you to reduce your stress. In this photo, best-selling novelist Barry Eisler presents naked at TEDxTokyo by getting close to the audience. (Photo: Patrick Newell.)

Les Posen

Les Posen is a Clinical Psychologist practicing in Melbourne, Australia. Using his knowledge of the brain sciences, he brings his understanding of neuroscience to help presenters deliver their best possible presentations.

http://lesposen.wordpress.com

Dealing with the Fear of Speaking

You've prepared your slides according to the new rules of presenting, you have great content to share, and you've emailed your bio to the conference hosts. All is ready for your next great presentation.

Yet, as you prepare for a real-time rehearsal to check your timings, that familiar feeling in the pit of your stomach revisits. Not again, you think. Popular public speaking books and web sites repeat the statistic that people are more afraid of public speaking than dying. While it's comforting to know you're not alone, in the end, it really doesn't matter: It's your problem and there is something you can do about it. Let's start with some neuroscience of fear.

Starting about 60,000 years ago, our brains developed a marvelous system of providing us with remarkable defenses against environmental threats. Sometimes, those defenses are set-and-forget types, such as automatically blinking when a bug hits your windscreen, even though you "know" you're protected. Other times, an evolutionary newer part of our brain where we make decisions and plans—the part that makes us most human—warns us of an upcoming threat. In the case of presenting, it might be fears of not connecting, or of our ideas not being accepted, or of going blank in front of 500 pairs of eyes. In historical terms, we still possess the fear of what it means to be stared at by so many people: Either we are the monarch, or more likely, we are the next sacrifice! Through evidence-based research and practice, clinical and performance psychologists have developed ways to help suppress these learned and ingrained fears, especially when we know we can perform well if only we give ourselves the chance.

There are five interventions I teach and want to share with you:

1. Chunking and exposure.
Identify and break down your presenting challenges into small manageable chunks, and deliberately expose yourself to each of them step by step.

2. Rehearsal.
Beyond just practicing your slide timings, actually visualize and hear yourself say the words with your slides. You see yourself in front of the crowd and rehearse your presentation to a variety of audience reactions, both positive and negative.

3. Self-talk.
Anxiety grabs onto self-critical talk such as "I'll do a terrible job. What happens if the slide show fails. What happens if they don't laugh at my jokes." Your task is not to feed your anxiety with this type of talk, but to change it into "I can do this. I will follow my rehearsed plans. This is manageable."

4. Arousal control via diaphragmatic breathing.
Calm your brain's fear center with slow, deliberate breaths with slightly longer exhales. Slower rhythm (rather than deep breathing) is helpful for fear management.

5. Deliberate practice.
Practice your beginning, identify challenging concepts, and practice, practice, practice—out loud. These techniques work, and I use them myself as well as with clients. They are powerful and will prove useful in scenarios other than presenting.

Inaction breeds doubt and fear. Action breeds confidence and courage. If you want to conquer fear, do not sit home and think about it. Go out and get busy.

— Dale Carnegie

In Sum

• There are many ways to strike quickly and start with punch to make a strong initial connection with your audience. Conveniently, at least five proven ways to begin a talk form the acronym PUNCH: Personal, Unexpected, Novel, Challenging, and Humorous.

• A presenter with good presence, just like a good conversationalist, will connect with you on some level. The speaker will demonstrate with sincerity that, at least for the moment, he or she does not wish to be anywhere else than right there having a dialogue with you.

• The three things to consider when evaluating your own ability to project yourself to your audience aside from the content of the talk are: the way you look, the way you move, and the way you sound.

There's more to enlightenment than how many facts you can recite.

— Neil deGrasse Tyson

4

Engage with Passion, Proximity, and Play

Standing up to recite information while others passively listen and perhaps take notes is the common and traditional presentation mode. But it's an ineffective way to teach, inspire, or motivate an audience. If the lone goal is the transfer of information, you are better off distributing a handout and canceling the presentation. When we finish a presentation, remember, we want the audience to be *changed*, if even only a tiny bit. We want to influence a change in people's knowledge, awareness, behavior, and so on. But unless we *engage* with the audience, none of that is possible. When there is no engagement, there is no change. True engagement assumes some level of emotional involvement or commitment on the part of both the presenter and the audience—but the responsibility to light the fire of engagement lies primarily with us, the presenters. This chapter looks at three elements involved in creating the kind of naked engagement we are looking for in today's presentations: Passion, Proximity, and Play.

Show Your Passion

In Japanese, the word passion—*jounetsu* (情熱)—is composed of two Kanji (Chinese) characters, feeling (情) and heat (熱). Although the etymological origins for the word may differ across languages and cultures, when you think of passion today, you immediately think of strong feelings and desires associated with love—love of another person, perhaps, but also a kind of love or deep feeling and intense emotion for a calling in your life like music, art, teaching, or whatever interests in your life evoke a strong and personal commitment. Passion is by definition a strong emotion with many associated feelings such as enthusiasm and vivacity. Emotions are a good thing, of course, but we have been taught to control our emotions in order to be successful in life. Much of this is good advice as there is a strong correlation between being able to self-regulate emotions and success in school, work, and life in general.

When it comes to presentation delivery, the problem generally is not the display of too much emotion but rather the utter lack of it. The emotions missing most from the dreariest of presentations today are passion and enthusiasm. Charlie Hawkins, public speaking consultant and author of *First Aid for Meetings* (Bookpartners, 1996), highlights the need for passion in a piece he wrote for sideroad.com:

> *While coaching hundreds of MBA candidates at the University of Chicago over an 11-year period, I observed that the one element separating great presenters from merely good ones is passion. Those who dared to express their passionate feelings about their subjects were consistently the most effective. Why? By revealing their passion they made connections with people that simply did not happen in straightforward analytical presentations.*
>
> *—Charlie Hawkins*

Sometimes a presenter may genuinely not have a passion for the topic or is greatly disinterested in sharing his ideas with the audience.

Often, however, the passion is lacking because the presenter is hesitant to project his or her emotion, true feelings, or true level of deep interest in the subject. Showing your passion—a true bit of yourself—is risky. It's much easier just to present information, but assuming people are still listening to you, what value do you add when you just give information?

Why are we afraid to show passion?

Many say that a man or woman who speaks passionately—who is articulate and full of hope, enthusiasm, and positivity—is an empty suit. They will say emotions do not matter. All that matters, they say, is content and evidence, period. Ironically, the very people who demand that content is everything and that emotion—and certainly passion—does not belong in "serious presentations" rail against the importance of emotion and engaging delivery in a manner that is completely emotional and heated. I know this because I have spoken to such people many times. They say it is simply the quality and structure of the information that matters—and that delivery and personal qualities, as well as things like simplicity and clarity in the design of visuals, are just not necessary.

The point that such people miss is this: Nobody ever said delivery, emotion, and passionate engagement are the only things that matter, or that they are sufficient. We only said they are *necessary* (and all too often lacking). Solid content is necessary as well, of course, but it's almost never sufficient in terms of leadership, communication, and presentations that have impact. If you are talking about trying to lead a movement, change the world, or just get your message heard and remembered, then you sure as heck better be prepared to show your passion. You don't have to be slick or polished, and you don't have to be tall or good looking, but you do have to engage, inspire, and motivate. That's what leaders do. That's what naked presenters do.

Passion is the genesis of genius.

— Anthony Robbins

Inspired by performers

Not too long ago, I was reminded about the impact of passion on communication by an unlikely source—a live performance by the legendary band Earth Wind & Fire here in Japan. We had seats (although we never sat) front and center, which allowed the perfect vantage point for observing one of the most passionate performers I have ever seen without a microphone. You may not have heard of him. His name is Verdine White, the bassist for EWF and an original member of the group, which was founded by his older brother Maurice.

White is an incredible musician with more funk and soul in his little finger than I have in my entire body. He is absolutely crucial to the EWF sound. But what White taught me that night was how unbelievably powerful a sincere display of genuine passion could be. White does not just play bass, he communicates and connects with his "ax" as if it were an extension of himself. White never stops bouncing, running, and seeming to fly across the stage all the while displaying one of the brightest, most infectious smiles you will ever see on stage. Oh, and by the way, he was 55 years old at the time. What energy!

They are musicians. They are artists. But they are also storytellers, and in a way, presenters while they are on stage. And like any good presentation, their performance is a powerful mix of great content, powerful visuals, and an emotional human touch that makes a lasting connection with the audience. The personal qualities that White's performance had—which our presentations must have—are: (1) passion, (2) energy, (3) sincerity, (4) a smile, and (5) total engagement with the present, front and center. How many times have you seen a presenter display all five of these qualities in a presentation?

We are deeply social animals, designed to be together. We create language and culture and come together to work, to dance, to play music, and so on. When you think about it, why is it we pay money to attend a live concert? We say it's for the music, but you can get the same music—with better sound quality—by listening to the CD at home. We're drawn to the live event in strong measure because it's a much richer experience when we can see the musician's faces and body movements and feel what they are feeling. The experience is enriched and more memorable when we can see and feel the performers' displays of passion.

Yes, an R&B/soul performance is different from a business presentation, but in a very real sense, they are both sincere performances. Dale Carnegie says the same thing in *How to Develop Self-Confidence & Influence People by Public Speaking* (Pocket, 1991). "Put your heart and soul into your talking. Real emotional sincerity will help more than all the rules." Carnegie also stresses the importance of exuding energy in your talk. "It is magnetic. People cluster around an energetic speaker like geese around a field of autumn wheat." Carnegie goes on to talk about the importance of smiling sincerely and displaying interest in your audience. "Like begets like," he says. "If we are interested in our audience...our audience will be interested in us."

We are naturally drawn to energetic presenters just as we are attracted to passionate performers.

Think interested not interesting

If presenters think about an audience at all, they usually worry about themselves not being perceived as interesting. However, the issue is not so much you showing how interesting you are—it's more about you showing how *interested* you are. We are attracted to people who are deeply interested in their work or topic and *also* interested in us. We like people who are interested in sharing their passion and interest in a way we can understand. People who are genuinely and deeply interested in what they are doing are demonstrating their passion. Interested people are the kind we want to listen to. Anyone can be more interesting superficially. But when someone is deeply interested, this brings us in and we want to know more. When they show they are interested in us, we are drawn closer.

Letting people know how and why you are deeply interested in the topic—and why they should be too—is very natural. People can see your passion and they can feel that it is real. This is very different from using performance techniques alone (such as speaking in a louder voice, emphasizing key words, using exaggerated body language) to demonstrate passion or to look more interesting than the typical presenter. You can't fake interest and the passion that accompanies it. So the question is not "How can I be more interesting to this audience," but "How can I demonstrate why this topic or information is important and how can I show why it matters to them?"

Tapping Emotions

Like it or not, we are emotional beings. Logic is necessary, but rarely sufficient when presenting. We must appeal to "the right brains" as well. The need to appeal to people's emotions is fundamental, yet often neglected. Here's what the authors of *Why Business People Speak Like Idiots* (Free Press, 2005) say:

> In business, our natural instincts are always left-brained. We cre-ate tight arguments and knock the audience into submission with facts, figures, historical graphs, and logic.... The bad news is that the barrage of facts often works against you. My facts against your experiences, emotions, and perceptual filters. Not a fair fight—facts will lose every time.
>
> — *Brian Fugere, Chelsea Hardaway, and Jon Warshawsky*

As presenters, we truly have a difficult job in trying to convince people to change their thinking or take new action. People tend to over-interpret their own personal and vivid experiences, and may ignore or remain very skeptical of new information—no matter how scientific or objective—that is contrary to their current beliefs.

Professor Richard Brislin from the University of Hawaii touches on a very similar phenomenon in his book *Understanding Culture's Influence on Behavior* (Wadsworth Publishing, 1999). Dr. Brislin discusses why people make dubious conclusions in spite of evidence to the contrary. For example, let's say you read many reports in respectable periodicals that conclude Seattle is a very good place for young graphic designers to find high-paying jobs. Complete with this evidence, you begin sending off your resume, contacting companies, and looking into housing in the Seattle area. Later, when you tell a friend, Lisa, about your desire to relocate to Seattle, she becomes practically apoplectic. "What?" she says. "My brother has a design degree from Berkeley and has been up in Seattle for over a year without finding a full-time design gig!" Lisa tells her brother's horror story of Seattle. So now you have the word of one friend versus loads of factual, detailed, documented information that runs contrary to your friend's opinion. Who do you believe? Citing early work on social cognition, Brislin suggests that it is highly likely you will be more persuaded by your friend's testimony, which was personal and more colorful, emotional, and vivid compared to the reading of labor reports in periodicals. And the fact that Lisa is "telling her story" about her brother makes her information more memorable.

We really have our work cut out for us. Our audiences bring their own emotions, experiences, biases, and perceptual filters that are no match for data and facts alone. We must be careful not to make the mistake of thinking that data can speak for itself, no matter how convincing, obvious, or solid it may seem to us. We may indeed have the best product or solid research, but if we plan a dull, dispassionate, "death by PowerPoint" snooze-fest, we will lose. The best presenters target both the logical left and the emotional right brains—that is, "the whole mind."

Each audience is different, though some are more skeptical than others. Regardless, a good presentation must appeal both to the audience's need for logic and for emotion.

Emotions and memory

If you can arouse the emotions of your audience with a relevant story, image, or piece of data that is unexpected or surprising—or sad or touching and so on—your material will be better remembered. When a member of your audience experiences an emotionally charged event in your presentation, the amygdala in the limbic system of the brain releases dopamine into that person's system. And dopamine, says, Dr. John Medina, "greatly helps with memory and information processing."

You can see the appeal to emotion in TV advertisements. A fantastic example of a 60-second spot that makes an impact and gets its message across by tapping into many different emotions is the award-winning Apple commercial called "1984." Regarded by many as the best and most memorable TV ad of all time, it ran during Super Bowl XVIII and introduced the Macintosh for the first time. Rather than trying to persuade the viewers with a logical argument that explains the benefits of the new type of computer, the commercial features an athletic heroine running to save the world from the scourge of conformity, which is represented by an Orwellian Big Brother talking head projected on a large screen in front of row after row of lifeless conforming subjects. While security guards close in on her, she is able to throw a sledgehammer over the heads of the seated conformists. The sledgehammer crashes into the screen, causing it to explode. The setting is industrial with dark blue and gray colors that contrast with the heroine's bright red running shorts and clean, white tank top featuring a subtle graphic of the Macintosh computer. The 60-second commercial exhibits solid conflict and contrasts and is filled with emotions ranging from sex appeal to threat to fear and surprise.

While your situation is not the same as making a 60-second advertisement, there is something to learn here. Ask yourself, for example, what it is that you're *really* selling. It is not the features or the thing itself. It's the *experience* of the thing and all the emotions related to it that you are really selling. Use stories and examples that are vivid and bring people's emotions into your narrative.

The power of emotional contagion

During a business trip to Denmark a couple of years ago, my friends and I spent a few hours in Tivoli Gardens in Copenhagen. This famous amusement park, built in 1843, apparently inspired Walt Disney when he was dreaming up his own famous amusement park. While in Tivoli Gardens, I received a strong reminder of something we all know but too often forget: that emotions are contagious and our emotional displays can and do influence those around us, often in ways we're not even aware of. We spent several minutes in an area of the park under and next to white-knuckle rides complete with screams and shrills—mostly of joy and excitement, but mixed with a touch of, perhaps, terror. Everyone on the ground was having a great time just watching the fun the other people were having on the attractions.

One of the attractions at Tivoli Gardens in Copenhagen.

It was a surprisingly enjoyable atmosphere; I could have spent much more time just sitting and watching the smiles, laughter, and displays of exhilaration of complete strangers. A grandmother sitting next to me got a real kick out of watching her teenage granddaughter and listening to her scream with excitement every time the ride whizzed by our heads. The grandmother was absolutely delighted. So was I. The remarkable thing was, even though I was not actually experiencing the excitement these strangers were having on the scary rides, I was feeling completely amused and happy by the displays of excitement and joy all around. The giddy emotion was utterly infectious and everyone in the crowd felt it. What we were experiencing that sunny afternoon in Copenhagen was a form of emotional contagion, which is the tendency to feel the emotions others are feeling and even mimic their facial expressions and moods.

Mirror neurons

In the last decade, based on earlier work at the University of Parma, Italy, researchers have gained good insights into something called mirror neurons. A mirror neuron is a neuron in the brain that fires both when you do something and when you simply see someone else doing the same behavior—even though you have not moved. It's almost as if you, the observer, are actually engaging in the same behavior as the person you are watching. Perhaps this is why watching sports is so captivating and compelling for most people. In a sense, we feel what the athletes are feeling. Watching something and doing something are not the same, of course, but as far as our brains are concerned, they're pretty darn close. We learn from watching others; we even learn bad habits from watching others. Mirror neurons fire when we see a behavior and also when we perform that behavior. So before we imitate a new behavior, our mirror neurons have already re-created that behavior in our brain.

Our brains are good at imitating actions, but just as importantly, they are really good at feeling what others are feeling. Mirror neurons may be involved in empathy as well. This is a crucial survival skill. Research has shown that the same area of the brain that lights up when a person experiences an emotion also activates when that person only sees someone else experiencing that emotion. When we see someone express passion, joy, concern, and so on, experts believe that the mirror neurons send messages to the limbic region of the brain, the area associated with emotion. In a sense, there is a place in the brain that seems to be responsible for living inside other people's brains—that is, to *feel* what they are feeling.

If our brains are activated by the movements and feelings of others, what does this suggest for the way we should present to a group of people? If we are wired to feel what others feel, is it any wonder that people get bored and disinterested when listening to someone who seems bored and disinterested themselves—even though the content may be useful? Is it any wonder why we feel stiff and uncomfortable while watching someone on stage barely move a muscle except for the muscles that make their mouth open and close?

We learn by watching and then by doing, but we also learn by feeling what others feel. Empathy and putting ourselves in another person's shoes allows a connection, and it is this connection that helps us to understand and learn. Yet much of presenting today in the overly formal, static, and didactic style removes the visual component, including the visual messages of our movements and the displays of our emotions. An animated, natural display of emotions surely enriches our narrative as it stimulates others to unconsciously feel what we feel. When you are passionate, for example, as long as it is perceived as genuine, most people to various degrees will mirror that emotion back.

The content of your message is crucial, of course, but others in the audience pick up on all sorts of other signals related to your emotional state. The best content in the world—with the best visuals in the world—can still be sabotaged by our emotions, that is, in how we influence others to feel. I have seen some technical presentations fail this year not because the content was irrelevant or disorganized, but because the presenter, due to inexperience or nerves, looked and sounded more like he was giving a particularly depressing eulogy rather than the results of an interesting piece of research. After 10 to 15 minutes of monotone and dispassionate narration, it becomes very difficult to stay with any speaker, regardless of the topic. Your story and your evidence matter, but the genuine emotions you project have a direct and strong influence—for good and bad—on the message your audience ultimately receives and remembers.

Power of the smile

For most presentation topics, a sincere smile can go a long way in helping to engage an audience. During a recent night in Osaka, Japan, I realized again the power a genuine smile has for connecting emotionally with an audience. I was inspired, in fact, by the person's smile, as were others in the audience—whether they were conscious of it or not. I was inspired not by a presenter but by a performer, Yoshida Miwa, half of the legendary Japanese duo Dreams Come True. Yoshida Miwa is the 46-year-old diva who fronts the group, a pop star with a great voice and a wide range with clear soul, funk, and jazz influences. Music aside, though, what I remember most about the three-hour concert was the infectious smiles of both Miwa Yoshida and her partner Masa Nakamura, the other half of the duo.

Smiles are indeed infectious. But the smile cannot be faked or forced. You can try to fake a smile, but people can tell when you don't mean it. In fact, some studies show that if you give an insincere smile, audiences may perceive you as untrustworthy or hypocritical.

Martin Seligman, author of *Authentic Happiness* (Free Press, 2004) says there are essentially two types of smiles: the "Duchenne smile" and the "Pan American." The Duchenne smile is the genuine smile, characterized by movement of the muscles around the mouth and also the eyes. You can tell a real smile by how the skin around the eyes wrinkles up a bit. The Pan American smile is the "fake" smile and involves voluntary movement around the mouth only. This is the polite smile you may see from someone in the service industry who is doing their best but not having a great day. We all can recognize an insincere smile. But a presenter or entertainer who actually looks like she is happy to be there—because she really is—is well on her way to engaging her audience naturally. A genuine smile shows that we are happy to be there. And since people in our audience can feel what we feel, why wouldn't we want them to feel at ease?

Whether it's a presentation or a performance, a genuine smile can go a long way toward making a genuine connection.

Some scientists, medical doctors, engineers, and others presenting on technical matters at a conference may dismiss the importance of the natural smile. They might say that smiling, rapport, and engagement are fine for marketers and general presenters, but serious people must be serious. Well, there is nothing unserious about smiling. Whether or not you use slides in your live presentation, your talk is still visual. And while you may think it's only your words that people should remember, the audience in fact will recall much of what they saw (including your facial expressions) and what they felt.

Interact Using Proximity

My experience teaching and presenting in different parts of the world for the past 20 years has taught me that the physical distance between a speaker and the audience—and between the individual members of the audience—has a great influence on one's ability to engage and be effective. The spatial context has a great impact on nonverbal communication and the quality of interaction, although this is often overlooked. The second "P" of engagement, then, is Proximity, a term inspired by Edward T. Hall's work in the field of proxemics, the study of how nonverbal communication among and between people is influenced by distance. What research in proxemics has shown is that variations in personal space and distance has an effect on interpersonal communication, and these effects may vary by individuals and by culture.

Most classrooms come with barriers. This student from Finland places the computer out front and moves away from the lectern to be closer to the audience and the screen.

Ideas concerning personal space may depend on culture, but as much as possible, presenting naked means you want to be close to your audience and you want members of your audience to be close to each other. There are physical limitations and each case is different, but as a general principle you should (1) shorten the distance between yourself and the audience, (2) bring individual audience members closer to each other while still being sensitive to local perceptions of personal space, and (3) remove any barriers between you and the audience that create distance, whether that distance is physical or merely a perception of the audience. Audience members might perceive distance, for example, if you use language that is too formal, inappropriate, or industry specific for a particular audience. Technology, too, if not used well can create a feeling of distance that diminishes engagement regardless of how close you may physically be to the audience.

Come out from behind the barriers

You may know Phil Collins as a singer, but he originally started out playing the drums. As his musical career progressed, he began to sing from behind the drums. In time, he came out from behind the drums completely and took center stage. Collins is a fantastic drummer, so when he performed recently on FM's Performance Theater, he was asked about the idea of singing lead vocals and playing drums at the same time:

> *Most songs are vocally driven. Yes, it is physically possible to sing from behind the drums…. But they want to see you. When you're behind a drum kit, it is very difficult to connect to people. That is why I am out in front.*
>
> *— Phil Collins*

In his early days with the band Genesis, Collins said singing from behind the drums was his "security blanket." Sitting behind the drums is indeed a pretty secure place to be. Karen Carpenter of the Carpenters was very hesitant to come out from behind the drums back in the '70s. It's scary to stand front and center, but that's where connection, engagement, and true communication live.

Physically, it's possible to sing lead vocals from behind the drums—and you can sound just as great—but what of the connection with the audience? Likewise, if you present from behind a lectern, you may, more or less, sound the same. And the media behind or beside you may look the same, but the connection is weakened. A lectern may be fine for a 15-minute speech at a university graduation ceremony, but it's a barrier in almost every other setting. For a situation where the people have come to specifically hear from you, to learn from you, and to be convinced or inspired by you, you need to do whatever you can to remove the barriers—literally and figuratively—between you and the audience.

For this presentation I remove the lectern and place the projector and computer together out of sight from the audience in the center of the room, leaving the front barrier-free.

Use a remote

If you are using multimedia that requires only a simple advance to the next slide (or next animation, start/stop video, etc.), which is all that most sequence-driven presentations require, then use the smallest remote control device you can find. The remote is an essential device that anyone who presents needs to own. There is no excuse for having to glue yourself next to a table or lectern just so you can use your fingers to advance slides. Having a small remote allows you the freedom to not only walk to different areas of a stage (or the front of the room) but to go into the audience as well.

If a presentation requires you to use your computer for more than simply advancing slides, then it's fine to occasionally go to the computer to start a program, demo a web site, and so on. However, you should also move away from that lectern when you do not have to be there. Hans Rosling, a doctor, researcher, and presenter, is extraordinary at doing this. When he needs to pull up some data or start the Gapminder program, he will occasionally go to his computer on stage. But Rosling also spends a lot of time near or in front of the screen explaining how to read the data or pointing out important points. Rosling is a technical presenter with passion; he is able to engage his audiences with the visualizations of data in part because he removes the barriers by often moving away from the lectern.

Hans Rosling removes the barriers and gets involved with the data, making things clear for the audience. (Photo: Stefan Nilsson.)

Performing demos

If you are performing a demo and you need to show how the software actually works, position yourself front and center so the audience can see you and the screen behind you. It's possible to keep a good connection with the audience while you use the computer—as long as you keep things moving and the conversation flowing. Apple's Steve Jobs is fantastic at doing this. Citrix CEO Mark Templeton is great at demoing his company's software in a friendly, engaging style as well.

The CEO of Tableau Software, Christian Chabot, is another high-tech leader who knows how to engage an audience with a demo. Chabot started his keynote at the company's 2010 annual customer conference in Seattle with a Gothic fairy tale complete with powerful imagery on screen. "The year was 2010," Chabot said. "It was a dark time for data." He then began to describe the current state of the business intelligence landscape, which included the evils of slow painful rollouts, explosive costs, and low user adoption (for people who didn't already use Tableau). Chabot told a dark story of user interfaces that included ancient wizards, complicated scripts, and the crumbling monolithic tower of the centralized data structure. After laying the foundation of where we are today, Chabot exclaimed, "People began to dream about a new way!" The CEO then unveiled Tableau 6.0 and showed the power of the new version and how easy it makes it to quickly query and analyze massive amounts of data.

Christian Chabot, CEO of Tableau Software.

While keeping his eyes mostly on the audience, Chabot took the audience through a journey of discovery that felt more like an interesting short documentary than a software demo. The key to Tableau is that it's a great platform for telling the story of data. Even though Chabot stood behind a lectern so he could demo the software himself, his demo was very compelling precisely because he engaged his audience in the manner of the passionate and friendly storyteller.

Technology should be invisible

Don't let technology or props take away from the experience. Very often in presentations given with slideware, we are all too aware of the software and computer. The technology should be as invisible as possible. While setting up, for example, don't have the screen on until your first slide is already in play mode. Many presenters actually allow the audience to see the computer screen boot up and then watch them mouse around for their PowerPoint file. This gives the audience the chance to glimpse the desktop picture of the presenter's cat before the first slide appears. How wonderful —and how irrelevant. All of this subtly takes away from the moment and purpose of the presentation, which is about the message and the story, not what software you are using.

The show must go on

Little mistakes can happen, but so what? Move on immediately to what is important. For this we can take a lesson from professional performers. For example, while attending a performance of Cirque du Soleil's Alegria in Osaka, I noticed one slip and gracious fall on to the net below during the Super Aerial High Bar. But the performance continued without missing a beat. The point was not the one slip— the point was to continue amazing the audience with the 1,000 other things that are going right. The audience does not even notice small mistakes; they often are too engrossed in the big picture. In a presen tation context, the audience does not know (or care) if you forgot to insert a slide or if the color is not as perfect as it was on your computer. Why dwell on the small imperfections? When small technical errors occur, you must go forward. And in the event that the technology fails completely, you must have a backup plan—such as speaking from notes sans visuals or speaking with the aid of a whiteboard. Remember, the show must go on even if your technology doesn't.

Sir Ken Robinson
on Public Speaking

Sir Ken Robinson is an educator and an expert on creativity. He's also one of the most popular TED presenters ever. His ideas on creativity and education—and his own personal presentation style—are truly an inspiration for many. Sir Ken does a lot of public speaking, almost always with no multimedia. During a podcast with the International Mentoring Network Organization, he spoke briefly on the issue of public speaking and presentation. A summary of his six major points on the subject of public speaking follows.

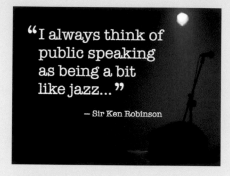

"I always think of public speaking as being a bit like jazz..."

— Sir Ken Robinson

1. Remember, you are speaking to individuals not an abstract group.
The size of the audience does not matter, says Robinson. You are always speaking to individuals. So speak as naturally to a large audience as you would to a small group.

2. Be as relaxed as possible.
People will feel relaxed if you are relaxed, so be as relaxed as possible, right from the start, to put the audience at ease. Seems like a small thing, but actually it is huge.

3. Be conversational and make a connection with the room.
But also keep the energy high. Being relaxed, natural, and conversational does not mean that your energy as a presenter should be the same as when you are chatting with friends in a cafe, however. Robinson says he gets a lot of energy from the audience so the connection is very important. If you have the connection and the energy (which is cyclical), then your impact and your message is more effective.

4. Know your material.

OK, this may seem a wee bit obvious, but then why do so many people use detailed notes? Partly it's due to nervousness, convention, or habit. But often it's because people are not fully prepared to be talking on the topic yet. If you know your material well, you should not need much more than a few bullet points on paper to remind you of the structure. Robinson says he thinks long and hard about his talks and writes down a few key bullet points on paper, not on screen. (A mind map on a piece of paper can also be a useful reminder and a road map for you; I sometimes use these.) Robinson never has extensive notes, just bullet points. If you know your material, you will be relaxed. If you don't, you'll seem nervous and this makes the audience nervous.

5. Prepare, but don't rehearse.

Think and plan ahead instead. There is nothing wrong with rehearsal, of course. Different people have different methods for preparing. But the danger in rehearsal is that it is possible to seem too rehearsed when you present. That is, you may seem too perfect, too inflexible, unnatural, and though technically perfect, you may lose the ever important natural connection with the audience.

6. Leave room for improvisation.

"I always think of public speaking as being a bit like jazz or the blues," says Sir Ken. He explained that he does not always necessarily know exactly what he is going to say, but he believes in stories. His presentation—like a jazz musician—is telling a story and he is taking people someplace. Yes, he has ideas in mind before he takes to the stage, but like a musician, he feels free to improvise. This is actually more natural and more flexible, and it enables him to engage more with each unique audience. Sir Ken Robinson also believes in humor, which he believes is important for stimulating creativity. And humor is good for getting people engaged with you and your message. "If they're laughing then they're listening," he says.

Make your visuals big

Nothing is more frustrating to an audience than being unable to see the information on your visuals because the elements are too small. When you project images that cannot be seen clearly by everyone in the room, this becomes a barrier and increases the feeling of distance. It also sends a message that the presenter is unprepared or does not care about the audience. You can shorten the distance if you remember to make sure you create the visuals that can be understood easily, without any eyestrain, from anywhere in the room. When it comes to visuals, think big.

Develop Play

We were born to play. Play is how we learn and develop our minds and our bodies, and it's also how we express ourselves. Play comes naturally to us. I was reminded of this while listening to a cool little jazz gig near the beach on Maui, Hawaii, in early 2010. I snapped the photo below of a little girl enjoying the simple beauty of that musical moment by dancing happily all by herself.

I love this picture because it shows both adults and a child at play. The adult musicians are expressing themselves through jazz, a complex form of play with rules and constraints but also great freedom—freedom that leads to tremendous creativity and enjoyment for the players and for the listeners. The child did not know or care about the complexities of the chords and the rhythms or the wonderful interplay among the musicians, yet the energy and beauty of the music made her smile, laugh, and dance. She did not care if her dance was "good enough"—she just danced because she was moved by the music. She danced with such exuberance and speed that she appears only as a blur in the photo. Dance is perhaps the purest form of play. Children move to music long before they receive instruction on how to dance. We are born to move and we are born to play. Children remind us of this. They remind us that we are passionate, expressive, social beings.

No matter what your age, play is important for learning, creativity, and innovation. Play makes us smarter. "Nothing fires up the brain like play," says psychologist Stewart Brown. "The thing that is so unique about our species is that we are really designed to play throughout our whole lifetime." You can be a serious professional or student and be playful. We need to think differently about play and realize that it is not the opposite of work. As Brian Sutton-Smith famously said, "The opposite of play is not work. It's depression." The playing skills we learned as kids are not superfluous, they are a necessity today.

We need trust to play and be creative, and trust is established through play signals such as a smile. We can use the tone of our voice, a facial expression, a gesture—all of these send subtle nonverbal signals and encourage playful engagement.

Overcome the Obstacles to Success

Budō, or the "martial way," is a term that encompasses the martial arts here in Japan. Bu (武) conveys the meaning "to stop clashing weapons." Dō (道) is "the way" or "the path" to truth and liberation. There is much we can learn by examining the principles found in traditional disciplines, even though they may seem quite removed from the daily experience of most people.

At the risk of greatly oversimplifying things, think of Budō practice as not only being about competition, fighting, and technique, but also about being a mastery of self. The items on the next page come from The Ten Evils for a Budō Practitioner, a list from a Kashima Shin School scroll that appears in the book *Budo Secrets* by John Stevens (Shambhala, 2002). These 10 items apply to one's character as a martial artist, but as the author points out, these are really aspects of ourselves that everyone needs to overcome. All of these evils are in us—we're just human after all—so the key is not to be defeated by them. Our enemy is not in the audience (or the competition). The biggest obstacle to success usually is not from without, but from within. I love these words by the late Aikido master Kensho Furuya: "You have the infinite capacity to do anything you want. You compare yourself to others—that's why you feel so limited."

The Ten Evils for a Budō Practitioner:

1. Insolence
2. Overconfidence
3. Greed
4. Anger
5. Fear
6. Doubt
7. Distrust
8. Hesitation
9. Contempt
10. Conceit

Although these may be within us, you can see how none of these 10 evils are helpful when making a presentation, performing a piece of music, or teaching a class. All of the 10 listed can be destructive and hold us back—fear and doubt, in particular. Fear holds a lot of us back. It is our fear of failure, our fear of what other people may think. We're afraid. We're not sure. So we hesitate, and we fail to act. Popular authors such as Seth Godin call this the Lizard Brain.

Confidence, meanwhile, is necessary and important, but overconfidence can sometimes be as destructive as fear. It can also hold us back. Overconfidence, conceit, and contempt also prohibit us from seeing the lessons from people and experiences around us. The old adage is, "Once you think you have arrived, you have already failed."

Humility, a virtue often gained through much practice, study, and experience, is key. Yet humility and great strength go hand in hand. A kind of projected modesty that is really a cover for self-doubt and fear, however, is not the same thing as humility. Genuine humility comes from a place of strength. It is the truly courageous who remain always humble. These are lessons we need not leave behind in the dojo. These are lessons for everyday life and work, including the work of presentation.

Play keeps us in the moment

A spirit of play engages us and brings us into the content and into the moment. Children remind us that we need more play in the classroom, the lecture hall, and especially the typical conference presentation. But first, we adults must give up the notion that play is not serious. We must abandon the notion that work (or study) and play are opposites. Work and play are inexorably linked—at least the kind of creative work in which we are engaged today and hope to prepare our children for. As designer and computer scientist Bill Buxton declared in his impassioned presentation at Mix '09 in Las Vegas, "You can not be anal. These things are far too important to take seriously. We need to be able to play."

Play is not anarchy, however. There are rules, especially for group play. Play also involves negotiation. There are rules about how and when to play. Old habits are hard to break, which is why we need some rules (for example, suspending judgment during a brainstorming activity) to break free from the habits that get us down and dampen the creative process. Shocking people out of their normal way of thinking and getting them to forget their "adult behaviors" for a while can lead to better ideas.

A spirit of play engages

Play creates a relaxed feeling of connection between the presenter and the audience and among the audience members themselves. Play fosters a collective experience of engagement with the content. That doesn't mean you shouldn't take the needs of the audience and the material seriously. It's important to take our work seriously, but we should be careful not to take *ourselves* so seriously. We do not need to be somber, especially during a presentation when we are trying to effect a change in people.

Good things happen when we stop taking ourselves so seriously. It's OK to have fun. It's OK to enjoy the experience and expose some of your true self without the doubt and worry about what other people will think. What would happen if you removed the fear? Play energizes. Do you want your audience to be energized or solemn? Or merely observe the established norms of formality?

Infuse play in your presentations

To instill a playful spirit, the presenter needs to create a secure environment. Tim Brown is the CEO of IDEO, one of the most innovative design firms in Silicon Valley and a company that understands the importance of play. According to Brown, children who feel the most secure in their environment are the ones who feel the most freedom to play. We can extend this to adults in the workplace as well. Fear—including fearing judgment from our peers—inhibits us and often prevents us from taking chances or sharing our ideas with others. Fear, says Brown, leads us to be overly conservative and to keep our "wild ideas" inside. As adults we become overly sensitive to the opinions of others and we lose a bit of our freedom. In presentations, we should create the kind of safe environments that encourages others to participate and take chances.

You can instill a subtle atmosphere of play by using humor naturally, as discussed in Chapter 3. Using humor naturally means relaxing, being your playful self, and interacting with your audience. You can point out irony, bust a myth, tell a story with an unexpected twist—anything that evokes a smile or a bit of laughter. Laughter is a fundamental social activity. When you laugh—and laugh together with others in your audience—you create engagement. In the best-selling book *A Whole New Mind* (Riverhead Trade, 2006), Daniel Pink identifies play as a key aptitude for success in a 21st-century world. Humor, of course, is a key component of play. "Humor represents many aspects of sophisticated thinking required in automated and outsourced times," Pink says. "And just plain laughter can lead to joyfulness, which in turn can lead to greater creativity, productivity, and collaboration."

A child's playful activities often involve exploration and experimentation. These are the very activities that some "serious" adults engage in as well, at least until they get up in front of a group of people to speak. As adults, we are too quick to categorize and put things in nice little boxes. We quickly come up with reasons why it can't be done rather than explore the possibilities and use our imagination the way children might. It's important, then, to encourage playful exploration and experimentation that contribute to a sense of discovery in presentations. Experimentation is crucial.

When you instill play by taking people on a journey of exploration, experimentation, and discovery, you arouse the brains of the participants and you just never know what you'll discover together. Discovery happens, after all, through a kind of play. Learning happens through a kind of play. And a playful spirit is opened to the possibilities. This is just as true for medical doctors and scientists as it is for designers, businesspeople, and teachers.

Children are natural explorers. But it's still in us. We can engage our audience by appealing to their natural attraction for discovery and exploration.

What is the role of entertainment?

Our society generally condemns the adults who dare play at work. People say play is simply entertainment, and therefore a passive and superfluous diversion. Many presenters resist the idea of bringing a playful spirit to their presentations. They may say that they are not in the business of entertaining. Their job, they will say, is simply to give the information and analysis, not to entertain. But there is nothing passive or distracting about a brain that is engaged, exploring, and discovering something new. Isn't an engaged brain in a sense an entertained brain? Perhaps the word "entertainment" has simply gotten a bad rap with the rise of informercials, infotainment, and the watered-down version of cable news networks that put sound bites, glitz, and pizzazz ahead of journalism and hard news.

We have to be careful with the term entertainment since it has many associations that serious businesspeople want to avoid. Its synonyms, after all, include distraction, diversion, and leisure activity—not what we usually think of in terms of business or academic presentations. But entertaining is also synonymous with many very appropriate terms, such as absorbing, affecting, compelling, delightful, engaging, engrossing, exciting, fascinating, inspiring, interesting, lively, moving, poignant, provocative, stimulating, and so on. We should be so lucky as to have an audience describe our presentations with one or more of these adjectives.

Nicholas Negroponte, the founder of the MIT Media Lab, is a visionary and driving force in the multimedia revolution. While speaking to an audience in Monterey, California in 1984 about the future of technology in education, Negroponte said, "Good education has got to be good entertainment." He is right—and this goes for most public-speaking situations as well. Anytime we are trying to teach, inform, and create a change in people, we need to entertain them. But you have to think differently about the word entertainment. By entertainment, I think Negroponte means engagement, meaning, and "personal involvement as well as activities that stimulate our natural curiosity and attraction to that which is novel and challenging. Education is knowledge and information. But the hunger, drive, and curiosity in the pursuit of understanding and meaning is emotional—it's human.

Many presentation situations—and education in general—have a lot in common since both can leverage the power of entertainment. The thing about being entertaining is that it is focused on others, the way it should be. It's not about us, it's about them. Different audiences are engaged and actively entertained in different ways. It's up to us to figure out what the most effective methods are for stimulating, affecting, and informing. Entertainment is not necessarily a distraction, diversion, or escape. In the best sense, entertainment is about engagement, connection, and meaning; it's about instilling a sense of play that opens minds and amplifies the engagement. You do not need to think of yourself as an entertainer or a performer, but virtually all solid presentations will be entertaining if targeted to the right audience. You say there are just some data sets that cannot be interesting (or revealing or provocative)? Then, as the saying goes, perhaps you have the wrong data (or the wrong audience).

Children need play to develop healthy brains. Everyone gets that. But the need for play is not limited to children. We'll have better and more empowered lives if we don't think in terms of a work-play differential. Rather than view play as something we do only outside of work time, we should instead live a life that is consistently infused with the myriad transformational dimensions of play.

Bringing a spirit of play to your presentations—and the feeling of exploration and discovery that it instills in the moment—improves learning and stimulates creative thinking. But often it's good to play for no other reason than to have great fun and feel good and recharged. We can find inspiration in play itself, and we are inspired by those speakers who understand that play is too important not to bring to work and include in presentations.

In Sum

• You can't fake interest and the passion that accompanies it. So the question is not "How can I be more interesting to this audience?" but "How can I demonstrate why this topic or information is important and how can I show why it matters to them?"

• Our story and our evidence matter, but the genuine emotions that we project have a direct and strong influence—for good and for bad—on the message our audience ultimately receives and remembers.

• As a general principle we must (1) shorten the distance between ourselves and the audience, (2) bring individual audience members closer to each other while still being sensitive to local perceptions of personal space, and (3) remove any barriers between us and the audience.

• Bringing a spirit of play to your presentations—and the feeling of exploration and discovery that it instills in the moment—improves learning and stimulates creative thinking.

No one is obliged to be a genius, but everyone is obliged to participate.

— Philippe Starck

5

Sustain with Pace and Participation

In my first three years of high school, I was a wide receiver for the football team and a sprinter on the track and field squad. In my senior year, I gave long-distance running a go for the first time. I was never very good at long-distance running compared to running much shorter distances in previous years. Whether I was running 5K or 10K, I always started too fast. I thought it was important to use all my nervous energy to make an impressive start, so once the gun went off I just couldn't help bolting from the starting line. The problem was I could never sustain the pace at which I started and I would eventually start to fade as the race progressed. This is when the meaning of "pace" really began to sink in. It didn't matter how well I started; I had to sustain that energy throughout the race.

At some point in our lives, most of us have been told to remember that life is a marathon, not a sprint. Although it sounds like a cliché, we know the essence of the old saying is true. The idea of pacing yourself and varying the speed and flow is important when presenting to audiences as well. This chapter looks at two elements involved in sustaining engagement with an audience: Pace and Participation. Getting people involved and thinking of them more as active participants rather than passive listeners is one of the keys to adjusting the pace and keeping people engaged.

Vary the Pace

Stand-up comedians are the quintessential naked presenters. What they do is scary. Few things are riskier and more difficult than standing with nothing but a microphone in hand in front of a crowd of people who expect you to make them feel something—that is, to make them laugh. Good stand-up comics masterfully connect and engage with an audience by telling stories, making observations, and sharing a bit of themselves that is real and genuine. "The best comedians in the world," says American talent manager George Shapiro, "are the ones who get their material from their heart and soul." This is true for the best presenters as well.

Now, you and I do not have to be funny, but we do need to evoke and to engage, something stand-up comedians know very well. In the documentary *Comedian*, Jerry Seinfeld touches on the importance of sustaining a connection with the audience and establishing good pacing. "You always need to establish yourself, establish the audience." In time, says Seinfeld, "You learn how to open, how to sustain, and how to pace." Even if we are able to make a strong connection and engage our audience initially, we still need to keep them engaged throughout the talk. Sustaining that energy and connection we made in the beginning is a matter of pace.

Unless you are attending the *Rocky Horror Picture Show,* watching a movie is a physically passive affair, and yet good movies sustain an audience's attention for two hours or more. How do they do it? In the case of a movie, the medium doesn't change. Instead, the story itself and the action and dialogue on screen appeals to our innate love of contrasts, often including variety/sameness, certainty/uncertainty, predictability/mystery, new/old, and on and on. In a movie, a central question or conflict is introduced early on and audiences stay with the events on screen until the question is answered or the conflict is resolved. A plot may be simple but the flow moves forward and gives the viewer the sense that he or she is part of a journey, or at least a witness eavesdropping on something remarkable. The intensity of a movie varies with the placement of provocative and evocative moments that move quickly and are juxtaposed with slower moments that provide a calm, contemplative break.

You may not be as seasoned at sustaining audience engagement as a great screenwriter or filmmaker, but you can learn from them. You can learn how their stories and delivery incorporate varieties of pacing and flow, not in an arbitrary manner but in a way that both contributes to the story *and* satisfies the audience's need for variety and change of pace. Aside from the structure of the narrative, there are many ways you can keep the audience engaged by adjusting the pace of the presentation delivery.

Attention and the need for change

When it comes to pace, the key word is change. To keep an audience engaged, you should have compelling changes in the content of our narrative (such as the sequential flow of a story), and you've got to change how you deliver your messages. Variety is the spice of life, the saying goes, and audiences are better able to pay attention if you build variety and change into your presentations. Attention spans are short by nature, and they are getting shorter given the plethora of distractions competing for the audiences' attentions. Granville Toogood cited a 1970s' study by the U.S. Navy in his book the *Articulate Executive* (McGraw-Hill, 1996), which found that the average time students could pay close attention during a lecture or presentation was just 18 minutes. My own experience tells me that the average attention span of an audience is much shorter than 18 minutes today, and the amount of time people are willing or able to endure a speaker they find boring is pretty close to zero minutes.

Dr. John Medina says we only get a few seconds to get someone's attention "and only 10 minutes to keep it." An animated, energetic lecturer, Medina was named the Hoechst Marion Roussel Teacher of the Year for his teaching ability and skill at keeping audiences engaged. According to Medina, after 10 minutes attention takes a nosedive—so a speaker has to do something different. "Since the 10-minute rule had been known for many years," Medina says, he decided that his lectures should be broken into modules, each lasting just 10 minutes. Following this method, one could get through about five modules in a typical class period. Medina recommends beginning each module or 10-minute segment by explaining a core concept in general terms to give people the big picture, then spending the majority of the 10-minute segment providing details that support the core idea. After about 10 minutes, however, you have to do something to change things up to keep people engaged. For this, Medina suggests you introduce an emotionally competent stimulus (ECS) that gives the brain a break and serves as a hook that connects one module to another. These hooks must be relevant to the material and, of course, they must be emotional. It could be a story, a video clip, a case study, an image projected on screen, or even a relevant amusing anecdote— anything that is relevant and triggers an emotion such as happiness, sadness, fear, nostalgia, incredulity, or any other human emotions.

The brain needs a break. Shift gears about every 10 minutes and consider introducing "emotionally competent stimuli" to increase engagement with the material. (Photo in slide above by iStockphoto.)

Varying the rate, volume, and pitch of speaking

It's usually good advice to slow down the rate of your speaking. Many novice presenters speak too fast, a reaction to the increased adrenaline running through the body. When a presenter speaks rapidly, the pitch increases and words may slur together, making understanding more difficult, especially for non-native speakers. In addition, audiences generally regard rapid speaking on stage as less powerful. Well-known and powerful business leaders such as Steve Jobs and Carlos Ghosn speak at a comfortable pace, neither too fast nor too slow.

In addition to the rate of speaking, you also want to naturally vary your volume. Remember, projecting does not mean shouting. There are times, however, when your volume can be quite loud as long as you contrast this naturally with softer parts that can still be heard. When you quiet your speech temporarily, people pay closer attention as if the softened speech indicates an especially important point.

A natural variation in your pitch (the highs and lows of your voice) is compelling. Natural variations in pitch are interesting—and that is why few things are more boring to us than listening to someone read a speech in a monotone voice void of emotion. Part of the reason for our boredom is that the dynamic range—the range found in a passionate, thoughtful, engaging presentation (or conversation), and the imperfect but real tone of someone speaking extemporaneously with enthusiasm and heart—is lost. A monotone lacks the inflections that affect the meaning of our speech. For example, inflections can stress important words and key points, which helps people to understand you better. Most novice presenters find that their pitch gets higher due to nervousness. A voice that is too high-pitched can be irritating and distracting. In Japan, I once saw an American presenter who was so nervous that his normally low and soothing voice sounded like he was taking hits of helium from behind the lectern. On top of that, every sentence ended on a high-pitched note as if it were a question: "Hello? I'm happy to be here? Thanks very much for coming? I'd like to start with a story? This is a remarkable story?"

Compelling speakers also make good use of silent spaces and pauses. Even if at times you find it difficult to avoid speaking rapidly, your impact can be greatly enhanced if you remember to insert silent pauses at appropriate places in your narrative. There is immense power in silence during a speech, just as there is in music. Just as the empty spaces (negative space, or white space) in visual forms of expression can make or break the effectiveness of the design, silence creates space for your words to breathe and have more impact. In a sense, where there is no quiet, there can be no loud, and where there is no nothing, there can be no something. We are drawn to the contrasts. The natural variations in rate, volume, pitch, and use of silence all serve to increase clarity and enhance engagement.

To really get a handle on how your own voice comes across, you need to take a video of one of your talks or presentations. You may be very surprised. Once you see for yourself that your pace was too fast and your pitch too high, for example, you will be better able to remind yourself during your next live talk to relax and project with energy—but in a manner closer to your natural conversational style in terms of pitch and speed of delivery.

Changing the Play

Being fully aware and mindful of your current presentation situation can also leave you open to possibilities for changing pace. For example, even though you have prepared a wonderful presentation and put a lot of time into designing the message and multimedia, there are surely times when even the best slides and brightest projector are just not appropriate. Sometimes, it may be better to just leave your cool MacBook or Vaio in your bag. Take a lesson from the best quarterbacks in American football—sometimes, it's best to just toss your plans and "call an audible."

Good presenters are like good quarterbacks: they are good at reading the situation live and making adjustments on the spot. Quarterbacks (QBs) are not usually the best athletes on the field, but they are skilled at reading situations and being able to change plans under great stress. When the offense approaches the line, a plan (a "play" called in the huddle) is already set. But as the QB surveys the defense before him, he may see threats or opportunities that require changing the play on the spot. The QB then yells special code words or signals down the line—to the left and to the right—so that his players know the new play. The QB uses the facts before him to make adjustments, but sometimes the decision to call an audible is based on a gut feeling for the situation. Some of the greatest plays ever have resulted from the QB calling an audible and changing the play at the last minute. Some of the greatest failures have resulted from the QB failing to adjust to the defense before him as well.

Image in slide from iStockphoto.

Adjustments matter. But adjustments require full awareness of the here and now and a flexibility to change.

Shortly after I started at Apple, I presented to a user group in California and had to call an audible. I had prepared a slide presentation on marketing and branding of organizations, such as user groups, for this particular audience. I was really looking forward to the presentation and took care to make sure the visuals were in line with Apple's standards. But when I arrived at the venue, the lighting, acoustics, and overall look and feel of the room were not what I had imagined. Nonetheless, I set up the equipment as planned.

I mingled around and talked to many members before the presentation. They were gracious hosts, a common characteristic of Apple user groups. During this time I realized that my prepared talk—as good as I thought it was—was not going to be a good fit for this particular group. I was disappointed, but was determined to push ahead with my presentation. After all, I was from Apple and people expect a kind of "mini-me" version of a Steve Jobs presentation, don't they? Still, somehow the projector-and-computer accompaniment did not feel right for the context.

At the moment I was introduced, I called an audible and changed my plan: I put down the remote control and pulled up a stool and sat down in the center, close to the front row, and proceeded to have what amounted to a fireside chat about Apple, user groups, the group's needs, their complaints, and so on. I listened as much as I talked during the hour. As I thought, the questions were quite different from the material I had prepared. Going completely "analog" in this case was a much better approach for this particular case. Even the best slides would have been a barrier to engagement and real conversation.

Less is more

Simplicity means removing the superfluous and keeping only what is essential. This is a fundamental design concept that applies to communication in general. Many presenters fall into the trap of thinking that, in order for their audience to understand anything at all, they have to tell them absolutely everything they know about the topic. So they rush through the material, making sure to cover a predetermined laundry list of points in hopes that something will stick. The trick, however, is in knowing what to leave out and in delivering your message in the simplest way possible without dumbing things down or being simplistic. The key is choosing the rights words—there are no prizes for those who speak the most words. It's about quality not quantity, and it's always about clarity. As Dizzy Gillespie once said, "It's taken me all my life to learn what not to play." The temptation to add more "just in case" is strong, but the brain needs a break. By removing the extraneous and speaking simply with an economy of words, you make things clear and keep the flow moving forward.

Use the B key

If you use slideware in your presentation, one of the most useful keys to remember is the B key. If you hit the B key in PowerPoint or Keynote, the screen goes black (pressing the W key, meanwhile, creates a white screen). You can even build black slides into a presentation to completely shift attention away from the screen. Pressing the B key is very useful, for example, if a spontaneous but relevant discussion diverges a bit from the visual information on the screen. Changing the screen to black removes the information, which may have become a distraction, and it puts all eyes on you and the people engaged in the discussion. When you are ready to proceed with your prepared points, just hit the B key again (this feature is on most remote controls as well) and the slides can be seen again.

Never go over time

When you speak past your allotted time you show disrespect for your audience. No one ever complains when a presentation finishes a bit early, but plenty of people will complain (at least to themselves) if you go long. I always urge people to embrace the Japanese idea of *Hara Hachi Bu*. This is a traditional dietary principle that means "eat only until 80 percent full." A traditional Japanese meal has great variety and an emphasis on fresh vegetables, rice, and seafood. And unless you are training to be a sumo wrestler, it is generally good form *not* to stuff yourself to the point that you cannot eat another bite. There is no reason to stuff yourself. By leaving just a little bit of room for more, most people find that they are actually quite happy and satisfied and feel much better after the meal.

Hara Hachi Bu is a proven general principle for increasing the quality and length of one's life. Showing restraint—not allowing yourself to continue to the point of being full—applies to meetings and presentations as well. It is much better to finish a bit early and have the audience wanting more than to wear out your welcome by stuffing your audience to the point of satiation. If your audience is satisfied and yet just a little bit hungry for more, then you know you have done your job.

Involve Through Participation

David Sibbet is the Zen master of visual thinking for groups. Sibbet's theory of meetings is that they should be truly interactive, collaborative affairs that are focused on participation. In his latest book, *Visual Meetings*, (Wiley, 2010) Sibbet says that "engagement is all about participation.... Thus the art of engaging begins with listening and establishing a connection and rapport." When we are trying to move people forward and effect a change, it is usually helpful to do things that get audiences involved. "People are much more apt to accept and implement ideas that come from within their group than ones imposed from outside—even by experts," he said. Sibbet is a facilitator who gets people to flesh out their own ideas and achieve clarity through a process of visual thinking and the participant-driven visualization of ideas. By the end of one of his seminars or meetings, the walls of the room are plastered with large sheets of paper that include sketches, maps, and collages that the participants generated. These graphics visualize the discussions that took place and lead to further discussion and collaboration. The visualization process increases involvement in a big way.

You may be presenting for only 20 minutes or an hour—and not have the time or tools for a collaborative activity on such a large scale—but the principle of Sibbet's approach to meeting facilitation can still be applied to the art of presentation. That is, as much as we can, we need to have the audience involved, participating, and *doing* something.

Have the audience do something

Confucius said, "I hear and I forget. I see and I remember. I do and I understand." Benjamin Franklin said something similar: "Tell me and I forget. Teach me and I remember. Involve me and I learn." If we learn by doing, why is there so little doing? Presentations, lectures, and class lessons are ephemeral and short. As much as anything else, shouldn't we stimulate people in a way that inspires and encourages them to go out and discover more about the topic on their own—at their pace and in a way best suited for them? Bullet point slides, for example, rarely inform, are hardly ever memorable, and never inspire action (unless that action is taking a nap).

Giving the audience an experience, one in which they do something, is important. In a 2009 podcast with the web site Lab Out Loud, famed astrophysicist Dr. Neil deGrasse Tyson—one of my favorite pubic speakers and a man who has been called the "Carl Sagan of the 21st century"—said this about the importance of experience:

> To experience something has a far more profound effect on your ability to remember and influence you than if you simply read it in a book. So why not figure out a way to turn a lesson plan into a living expression of that content. A living expression, so that sparks can be ignited and flames can be fanned within the students. And at that point, it doesn't matter what grade they get on the exam because they are stimulated to want to learn more. If they didn't learn all the 'A' stuff for that exam, they're inspired enough to go out and buy a book or spend more time on the documentary that they saw on the Discovery Channel or on PBS. And there it is. You've cast a learner into the world. And that's the most powerful thing you can do as a teacher. The enthusiastic teacher is fundamental to igniting flames of interest in any student in any subject. That's a need for all teachers in all subjects.
>
> — Dr. Neil deGrasse Tyson

Dr. Tyson is talking about education and the classroom, but we can apply his principles to presentations in a much wider context. A dull lecture has never been optimal, but the students and professionals of today are faced with far more distractions and dynamic media than past generations. Listeners have the responsibility to do their best to pay attention and live in the moment, but you have the ultimate responsibility to get them involved and ask them to participate.

Offer an "aesthetic experience"

Speaking recently on the topic of education to the Royal Society of Arts in London, Sir Ken Robinson touched briefly on the dangers of penalizing students for getting bored and distracted—even medicating many of them for ADHD to calm them down and help them focus. It's not that ADHD is not real, he said, but that it is not the epidemic it is made out to be. Sir Ken then went on to use the example of the arts to stress the importance of involving all of the students' senses and providing rich experiences for them from which to learn:

> The arts especially address the idea of aesthetic experience. An "aesthetic experience" is one in which your senses are operating at their peak. When you're present in the current moment. When you're resonating with excitement of this thing that you are experiencing. When you're fully alive. An 'anaesthetic' is when you shut your senses off and deaden yourself to what's happening.
>
> We're getting children through education by anaesthetizing them. And I think we should be doing the exact opposite. We shouldn't be putting them to sleep, we should be waking them up to what they have inside themselves.
>
> — Sir Ken Robinson

We don't usually think of "aesthetic experience" when we think of presentations, lectures, or public speaking in general. But why not? A presentation or public speech absolutely should be an aesthetic experience. We should be so lucky as to have our audience fully alive and in the moment with us—to have their senses totally engaged with our message, a message that resonates and encourages participation. Public speaking and teaching is not fine art, but there is an art to it. When we engage with an audience in a manner that generates connections, participation, and conversations that effect change, that activity is far more art than science. And while each audience member or student has a personal responsibility to make an effort to understand, it is our responsibility to "wake them up to what is inside themselves." We need to do this by creating content that is relevant, including them through participation and dialogue, and delivering material in a passionate way that stimulates their senses and emotions (such as curiosity and amusement, the kind of amusement or delight gained through discovery and learning something new).

Conversational language invites participation

You can't always have the audience do something physically, but you can still invite them to participate by speaking in a human voice and using a conversational language, a subject touched on in Chapter 1 as well.

Kathy Sierra, popular speaker and co-creator of the award-winning Head First series of computer books, says that our brains want a conversation. The Head First books do a unique job of presenting instructional and technical information in a visual, conversational, and compelling way. Although I am not much interested in writing software code, years ago I purchased *Head First Design Patterns* simply because it is such a good example of presenting potentially "dry technical information" in a way that is engaging without being dumbed down.

Whether we are reading a book or listening to a lecture, a conversational approach with the reader or listener is often the best approach. "The more advanced the topic," Sierra says, "the more you need to pull out all the stops in trying to make it more understandable."

What Sierra means is that when you present information in a conversational way, the listeners' brains think they are in a conversation and that they have to hold up their end of the conversation by paying attention. Conversations, after all, are not one way. Admitting that it is a bit of a generalization, Sierra says, "If you're using formal language in a lecture, learning book (or marketing message, for that

Presentation Tips from a Steve Jobs Keynote

Apple's Steve Jobs is a good example of someone who presents with the help of multimedia in an engaging style. It's true that he has great products to talk about, but he is also incredibly skilled at presenting those products. Great content is a necessary condition, but it is not sufficient. Jobs has both solid content and excellent delivery skills. Given his fame and exciting, sexy products, you may think that his presentations are relatively easy

Photo credit: Gail Murphy

to pull off. But the opposite is true. Because of his reputation, the expectations for each of his keynotes are very high, making it almost impossible to surpass expectations. As someone quipped after a Jobs keynote a few years ago, "If Jobs had announced contact with an alien civilization, it wouldn't have 'shattered expectations.'" The downside of having a reputation for being "insanely great" at anything is that expectations will surely rise for you to top your last perfor-mance (your last product, your last album, your last book, etc.). This is a good problem to have, but it is a real challenge nonetheless. I have written about Jobs's presentation style on the Presentation Zen web site for years. Here are just a few of the lessons we can take away from his presentation style.

• **Develop rapport with the audience.** Jobs usually walks out on stage, all smiles, without any formal introduction over the PA. Jobs shows his personality, which is confident but humble, on stage. People are attracted to confidence—but it must be confidence combined with humility. He uses natural movement on stage, eye contact, and friendliness to establish a connection with the audience.

• **Give them an idea of where you're going.** You do not need the ubiquitous and infamous agenda slide, but give people an idea where you're going, a road map of the journey you're taking them on. In Jobs's case, he may give a simple welcome, build a little rapport with a humble thank you, and then boom! "I've got four things I'd like to talk about with you today. So let's get stated." He may not say what the four things are, but just knowing that there are four major parts helps the audience. Jobs often structures his talks around three or four parts with one theme.

• **Show your enthusiasm.** You may want to curb your enthusiasm at times, but most presenters show too little passion or enthusiasm— not too much. Yes, a presentation on medical treatments by a researcher is different than a CEO's keynote. But in each case the appropriate level of enthusiasm can make all the difference. In just the first few minutes on stage Jobs may use words such as incredible, extraordinary, awesome, amazing, revolutionary. You can disagree with him. You can say his language is over the top; you can call it hype if you want. But Steve Jobs believes what he says. He is sincere. He is authentic. The point here is not to be like Steve Jobs but to find your own level of passion and bring that honest enthusiasm out in your work for the world to see.

• **Be positive, upbeat, humorous.** Jobs is a very serious person, but he is very enthusiastic because he really believes in his content. He is upbeat and positive about the future even in bad times. You cannot fake this—you must believe in your content or you cannot sell it. Jobs also brings a little humor to his talks. This does not mean telling jokes. His humor is more subtle. Making people laugh with relevant, subtle uses of irony is engaging.

- **It's not about numbers, it's about what the numbers mean.** A business keynote by a technology company is different from a scientific presentation at a conference. But isn't it always about what the numbers mean rather than just the numbers themselves? So your cholesterol is 199, the national average. Is that good or bad? Up or down? Is "average" healthy or unhealthy? And compared to what? When Steve Jobs talks about numbers in his keynotes, he often breaks them down. For example, he may say that four million iPhones sold is the equivalent of "20,000 per day" since the units went on sale. 20 percent market share? In and of itself that does not mean much, but the meaning becomes clear when he compares it to others in the field.

Photo credit: Macworld.com

- **Make it visual.** Jobs uses huge screens and large, high-quality graphics. The images are clear, professional, and unique, not from a template. Charts and graphs are simple and beautifully clear. There is no "death by bullet point." He uses the screen to show visual material and only occasionally for displaying short lists. He displays data in a way that the meaning is clear.

- **Introduce something unexpected.** Jobs's presentations, of course, always have something new. But he also surprises audiences just a bit each time. Humans love the unexpected. We love some element that makes us go "aah!" The brain loves novelty and the unexpected.

• **Include only what is necessary.** Jobs separates his talks into clear sections, usually no more than three. He makes a clear decision not to include too much. You cannot say everything; you must choose what is most important for now and leave the rest out. Most presentations that fail do so because they include too much information and display it in a cluttered way that does not engage the brain.

• **Vary the pace and change techniques.** Jobs is good at varying the pace from fast to slow and changing the flow by using different techniques. He does not stand in one place and lecture, a very bad way to present. Instead, he mixes in video clips, images, stories, data, different speakers, and live hardware and software. Just talking about information for one or two hours is much too boring for the audience (and for the presenter). If the talk is only about information and new features, it is more efficient to give that info out in a paper to read.

• **Save the best for last.** People will assess your performance in the first two minutes, so you have to start strong. But you have to finish even stronger. People best remember the first part and the last part of your presentation. The middle stuff is important, of course, but if you blow it at the start or at the end, all may be lost. This is why you have to rehearse your opening and your closing so much. Jobs is famous for his "one more thing" slide where he saves the best for last—after it appears he has finished.

• **Go the appropriate length.** Jobs never includes unnecessary details and makes it a point to finish on time. He is aware that presentations cannot go on too long and gets to his points smoothly and quickly. If you cannot explain why your topic is important, interesting, and meaningful in 20 minutes or less, then you do not know your topic well enough. Try to make talks as short as possible while still making the content meaningful, keeping in mind that every case is different. The key is not to fill your audience up; you want them wanting a little more.

matter), you're worrying about how people perceive you. If you're thinking only about the users, on the other hand, you're probably using more conversational language."

An overly formal and jargon-filled style can be a great barrier to communication and dissuade audience participation. On the other hand, a human voice that is natural, uncontrived, and open invites the audience members' brains to pay attention and participate. Your speaking does not have to be perfect. In fact, perfect speech and too much polish may alienate a crowd. It's not real. Each case is different, but an honest, friendly, relaxed approach—away from the lectern—is usually best. People pay more attention to a natural, open voice. Speak to the audience like you respect them and think they are smart and interesting.

How to get people to participate

Getting people to participate in your presentation adds variety to the pace, creates energy in the room, and makes your material more engaging and memorable. You want people to feel a part of the presentation somehow, not merely passive observers. You do not have to resort to tricks or gimmicks, but some very simple techniques can improve the overall richness and value of the experience by getting people to participate.

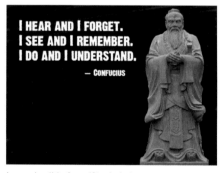

Image in slide from iStockphoto.

• **Ask questions.** Perhaps the easiest thing you can do is ask questions of the audience. "What do you think happened next?" or "How much do you think the Japanese yen has appreciated over the last five years?" Even if you are on a big stage and you can't really hear the audience, you can ask rhetorical questions that you then answer.

It's Not the Numbers, It's What They Mean

I'm a huge fan of Hans Rosling, the public health professor from the Karolinska Institutet in Stockholm and one of the cofounders of Gapminder (www.gapminder.org). Rosling is the Zen master of presenting statistics and one of the most popular speakers at TED. Rosling proves what we all know: Statistics are *not* boring. But Rosling shows that it is not enough just to show data—what matters is the *meaning* of the data. Statistics tell a story.

Photo of Hans Rosling by Stefan Nilsson.

The way the Gapminder software displays data is compelling and clarifies the data while bringing the viewer in for a closer look. It is, however, Rosling's delivery style that really engages the audience and allows them to participate and feel a part of the investigation of the data. Rosling is natural, funny, and passionate—he knows his points and where he's going with them. His graphics are easy to see and understand, but he still takes time before running the animation to explain the variables on the vertical and horizontal axes as well as the meaning of the size and color of the bubbles and such. As the animation progresses, Rosling explains the meaning of the movement as it is happening. He does this not by standing passively behind a lectern, but by moving closer to the screen and getting involved with the data and encouraging the audience to do the same.

When Rosling presents, it's not just the visualization of the data that is compelling. More importantly, *he* is compelling. He's adding value to the data display by adding context and meaning, and by emphasizing and pointing the way. Rosling shows his energy and engages the audience with the data by the way he speaks: "Do you see that? Look here! This is amazing! What do you think happens next? Wasn't that surprising?" and so on. It is not enough just to show numbers. If you are in front of an audience, tell them what you think the statistics mean, why, and compared to what?

Questions and answers do not have to be left to the end, especially when you are asking the questions. Throwing the occasional question out to the audience makes your talk feel more like conversation. Asking even rhetorical questions—such as "It's that amazing?" or "Wasn't that a surprising result?" for which you do not expect an actual verbal answer—shows that you are acknowledging the audience.

• **Show a video clip.** Showing short video clips that portray a real-life example, illustrate a point, or introduce a concept inserts a change of pace and adds richness to the experience. You can make the video even more engaging by asking the audience to watch for something in particular in the clip.

• **Show an image or quantitative display.** Visuals, when not used merely for decoration, provide loads of information and invite the viewer in to interpret. Visuals are particularly useful because, although we cannot read and listen at the same time, we are very good at listening and looking at relevant imagery. Increase the participative nature of the visuals by asking the audience to look for something specific, interpret the imagery, or provide their own analysis. Showing a series of images that displays contrasts—such as before/after or now/then—is a particularly strong way to engage the viewer. Images that evoke strong feelings are effective as well. As long as the imagery is relevant, the strong feelings the images evoke can increase attention and make the message more memorable. A flood in a distant land seems like an abstraction, but add high-impact vivid imagery of that flood and it becomes real and touches the viewer on a visceral level. In his 2009 TED talk, Information Designer Tom Wujec suggested we use images in three ways: (1) to clarify ideas, (2) to create engagement with our ideas, and (3) to augment memory with persistent and evolving views.

• **Take a poll.** I once saw a presenter begin her talk this way: "How many people in the room think there are more women than men in the world? Raise your hands. Thank you. Now, how many of you think there are more men than women in the world?" Most people in the room believed there were more women than men in the world—because in developed countries, that is largely true. The audience was very surprised that there are actually more men in the world. The presenter had their attention and involvement and went on to show some of the unexpected reasons for this statistic.

• **Use role playing.** Role playing can be used to experiment with nonphysical designs such as health-care services, educational settings, and so on. In general, we should take role playing more seriously (as children do). Role playing is important for putting ourselves in the shoes of the end users, and looking at the world and experiences from another's point of view. Role playing is an empathizing tool. Trainers and facilitators use role playing to simulate real-world situations.

• **Conduct quick brainstorming activities.** Proper brainstorming can take quite a bit of time. Instead, you can have an audience form small groups and perform shorter brainstorming sessions during which their only goal is to generate as many ideas as possible for a particular problem. In small groups people feel less intimidated to speak up so more people get involved. After a specified time, ask each group to narrow their list to three ideas and quickly share those with the audience or write them on the whiteboard for all to see.

• **Ask for a volunteer.** A common technique in show business is to ask for a volunteer from the audience to come on stage to participate in a demonstration. Using the help of a person to prove a point helps the audience feel a part of your talk. For example, when I teach about body language and personal space, I'll bring a few people on stage to demonstrate cultural difference in proxemics. This provides a real-life visualization of the concepts, brings the audience closer, and usually gets a lot of laughs, too, as a spirit of play is added to the demonstrations.

• **Have people build with their hands.** The things that facilitate playful building modes, hands-on learning, prototyping, and so on are abundant for young children in elementary school, but those opportunities are nearly nonexistent as children move through the education system in later years. The typical adult office is even worse (except for Post-it Notes and the rare, coveted red stapler). We need to be able to work out our ideas with our hands more. Designers call this "construction play"; children do it all the time. Adults can do this too; it's called "thinking with your hands." Given the constraints of your situation, what materials can you introduce that participants can use to prototype?

• **Sketching ideas.** At the very least you can get audience members to use their hands by sketching out ideas on paper. They can do this individually or in small groups. Sketching can be used for myriad problems. For example, participants could be asked to sketch plans for the ideal rail system for their city and then present their ideas to the group.

• **Use a game with a time limit to bring a sense of urgency.** While a strong emotion of fear can have a negative consequence on understanding, a playful sense of urgency increases arousal, attention, and recall.

• **Discussion groups.** If you are speaking to a large group, it is useful to break that group up into smaller groups and give them a problem to discuss. Clear objectives and a specific time are necessary. The brain needs time to process new information. Small discussion groups give people a chance to discuss the material in their own words and check with others for understanding.

• **Fill-in-the-blank.** In Japan, the Monta Method is a technique used by a TV personality named Mino Monta. This is just like the fill-in-the-blank test in school except that the sentences are written on a board and a piece of paper covers the answers. The audience tries to guess the answers. When the host removes the paper, it reveals an answer that is usually shocking and gets the whole audience involved, laughing or shouting out loud in surprise. This engagement and unexpectedness—along with the energy in the room as everyone tries to figure out the piece of the puzzle that is missing—makes the material more memorable.

Ten minutes into my seminar in Japan, participants stand up to do an activity related to the content. Note the placement of the computer close to the front and out of the sight of the audience. The large lectern was removed.

• **Use of case studies.** I sometimes give out short case studies called "critical incidents" that describe an actual intercultural encounter involving a conflict. Each group reads a different case study, then discusses the underlying reasons for the conflict and comes up with possible solutions. Then each group reports to the larger group, sometimes by acting out the incident and providing commentary.

• **Stimulate their imaginations.** Imagination is one of the most distinctive features of human intelligence, and yet most presentations do not ask people in the audience to use their imaginations or contribute their own imaginative insights. Give people hypothetical questions or ask them to fantasize and generate "wild and crazy" solutions to a particular problem.

In Sum

• The human attention span is short. To keep people engaged change the pace by doing something different about every 10 minutes or so. Introduce an "emotionally competent stimulus" to increase engagement and improve memory.

• Change the pace of your speaking and project a natural variation in tone. Remove extraneous words and speak simply with an economy of words. Be careful not to speak too fast; remind yourself to slow down when you are nervous.

• Show empathy by paying attention to how the audience is responding and be ready to change plans quickly to suit the needs of your audience.

• One way to sustain engagement is by getting people to participate. Ask people questions, show a video clip, do role-playing, or have a discussion activity—there are many ways to get people to participate. A conversational tone will also invite people in to participate with your you and your message.

There is a vitality, a life force,
an energy, a quickening that is
translated through you into action,
and because there is only one of
you in all of time, this expression
is unique.

— Martha Graham

6

End with a Powerful Finish

In Chapter 3, you learned that you must begin presentations with PUNCH—you must make a strong connection right from the start since, according to the *primacy principle*, people are more likely to remember what they experienced at the *beginning* of a presentation compared to what follows in the body of the talk. A strong beginning is crucial. However, a strong finish is just as important. The *recency principle*, a phenomenon where people focus on the most recent topic, suggests that people have a very strong tendency to remember what occurred at the *end* of a presentation compared to content delivered in the middle. We are generally pretty good at recalling the beginnings and the endings of presentations and other events. You know this is true from your own experience. If you look back you can recall the endings of your favorite movies or the last songs of a concert, but the middle bits may be foggy. Because the end of a talk has a disproportionate amount of salience for the audience, it is important that we finish with a bang. This chapter looks at ways that you can end your presentation powerfully.

Make Your Ending "Sticky"

All truly effective presentations are about creating a change in the audience. An ending is powerful to the degree that it helps your message resonate with the audience, thereby increasing the chance that the change takes root. When your ideas and your energy are transferred to others—causing them to make a change—we can say that your message has resonance. If your ideas resonated, your message will continue to inform, evoke feelings, and inspire action long after people have left the room and taken your message with them. Only it won't feel like *your* message—it will feel like *theirs*.

Sustaining a connection until the end and delivering a powerful finish, however, requires that you understand your audience well. In her fantastic best-selling book *resonate: Present Visual Stories that Transform Audiences* (Wiley, 2010), Nancy Duarte, CEO of the award-winning firm Duarte Design, says, "The audience does not need to tune themselves to you—you need to tune your message to them." Skilled presenters, says Duarte, understand the hearts and minds of their audience "...and create messages that resonate with what's already there."

One way to make certain your ending connects and is remembered is to make it "sticky." Sticky messages resonate. In 2007, Chip and Dan Heath wrote a best-selling book called *Made to Stick: Why Some Ideas Survive and Others Die* (Random House, 2007) that offers straightforward advice for making your ideas more impactful and memorable—in other words, more sticky. They found that the ideas and messages that stick the best contain six common elements: Simplicity, Unexpectedness, Concreteness, Credibility, Emotions, and Stories. These elements, which can be placed at various levels of your presentation, are especially applicable to your closing words. The stickier your message and delivery at the end, the more likely your messages will be remembered and acted upon. Let's briefly review the six sticky elements.

1. **Simplicity.** Never add more when less will do. Especially at the end of your talk, when the audience has already heard a lot, you must be ruthless in your efforts to simplify your last key message. Think in terms of having the maximum impact with the minimum means. Simplicity, say the Heath brothers, is "about elegance and prioritizing, not dumbing down." Make your ending as elegant as possible by removing the nonessential detail to reveal your final core point.

2. **Unexpectedness.** Earlier in your presentation you may have leveraged the power of unexpectedness to arouse people and get them curious. The ending might include that "aha moment" where you give the answer and insight to the puzzle you posed earlier. Perhaps you started with a relevant story with a mysterious and surprising twist. Now you can solve that mystery or guide them to the solution at the end. Another aspect of

Image in slide from iStockphoto.

unexpectedness that applies to the finish is to simply not end in the conventional way with saying something like, "Any more questions? No? Well, that will do it for me then. Thank you for your attention." Virtually anything you do other than this traditional boring "conclusion" will be a welcome surprise.

3. **Concreteness.** Many presentations fail because of too much abstraction. The ending is especially a time to make things clear and concrete. Avoid jargon and speak in clear, direct language. The ending is no place for muddled thinking or speaking. A final short example or very short story that illuminates your theme or key takeaway can work. A high-impact image projected on screen can also be effective at making the abstract more concrete.

4. **Credibility.** Your presentation is more credible when it has structure and you back up your claims with evidence and statistics—and more importantly, by putting statistics in their proper context and in terms people can visualize. Using a quote, a statistic with meaning, or a short video clip from a reliable, respected source that supports your core point are ways to end on a credible note. Other ways to gain and keep credibility are to show great respect for your audience by finishing on time, dressing the part, and using language that is friendly, open, natural, and also respectful.

5. **Emotions.** It is never just about information. If information was all the audience wanted, they could read your book, report, brochure, or web site. It is not enough to take people through a summary of your talking points—you must make them feel something (other than the pain of looking at your dreary summary slide). Make your ending personal, and make a link so that it is personal for your audience as well so they will care more. "The goal of making messages emotional," say the Heath brothers, "is to make people care. Feelings inspire people to act." Closing with a particular example or story is, again, a way of revealing the particular to emphasize the point of the general (your core point). People care about particular cases sometimes more than they care about a general pattern. Particular cases trigger their empathy and make your point more memorable. We remember better that which aroused our emotions. Images are, of course, an effective way to have audiences not only understand your point better but also to feel and have a more visceral and emotional connection to your idea.

6. **Stories.** Many people like to close with a final argument. The problem with that is, while you are arguing and making your case, the audience is looking for the flaws in your argument. In a sense, say the Heath brothers, you are inviting them to debate and argue back. There is a time for this, but not at the end. You are trying to get the audience members to go out and take an action. Story is not argument. A story invites people in to participate. Consider the kind of story that illustrates the problem you've been talking about and then shows a concrete, real solution. Stories are naturally engaging and memorable— they move people to action. If you want your ideas to spread, put them in the form of a story. Some of the best presenters open with a story and close with a story. An idea wrapped in a story is easier to repeat.

How to End on a Powerful Note

In whatever manner you choose to deliver your closing, do not retreat from the audience—get close to them. Walk to the center of the stage or the front of the room, slow your speech, look at individuals as you talk, and keep your energy high. Here are some ways to finish your talk.

Take it back to the beginning

Many presentations begin with the conclusion (the main point) right up front. In this case, it is easy to bring a harmonious close to your presentation by simply going back to your original point. If you started with a provocative story, you can go back to that story to show once again how the moral of the story supports your message.

Most presentations are less than an hour, but I often do seminars that last five hours or an entire day. For the seminars I did this year in Japan, I spent the first one or two minutes showing examples of famous and not-so-famous Japanese who have learned to be great presenters. Many Japanese think that Westerners can be good at dynamic presentation but—because their culture does not traditionally encourage it in business—they themselves cannot. After showing several examples and asking the question, "So, can you be a great presenter?" I show a slide on the large screen behind me that shows Barack Obama in Japan saying "Yes You Can!" This gets a big laugh from the audience and also gives the audience encouragement.

Five to eight hours later, after they have received a lot of information and spent time working together learning new skills and concepts, I wrap up the seminar with a very short summary. But that's not where I end. I finish by posing the same question I started the seminar with: "Can you be a great presenter?" As the same slide appears again with the words "Yes You Can!" in bold type, the audience says without hesitation: "Yes I can!" The seminar includes loads of information and principles that they studied. But more than anything else, I want them to be inspired and motivated to continue to study and learn on their own through future practice.

Summarize your main points

In school we learned that in public speaking we should (1) tell the audience what we will say, (2) say it, and (3) tell them what we said. When followed literally, this formula is a bit boring. Still, there is value in reviewing and summarizing. Repetition is an important part of learning, so a quick summary of key concepts has value—but don't leave it there. After a quick review, show or do something unexpected that reinforces a key point, or show an image you want people to remember that illustrates the core point.

Tell a story

Don't pile on more facts and statistics. Instead, tell a story or anecdote that encapsulates your core message. The best stories will have all of the sticky elements mentioned in the book *Made to Stick.* Keep it simple and brief, keeping in mind that the sequential nature of short story is very easy for audiences to follow, and the emotions that are evoked and the pictures that the story paints, helps make your message more memorable. Good stories have a moment of reflection in them. You may have opened your talk with a story that raised a question. You can now use another story—or an update of the same story—that answers that question.

Make them laugh

Yes, humor may be a little risky, but presenting naked has some risks. But humor itself is not as risky as jokes. Jokes—especially irrelevant ones—do not really have a place in most speaking situations. But a quirky example, story, image, or quote that is ironic, provocative, and reinforces a point while making people laugh, thereby allowing you to end on a high note, can be very effective. Take advice from professional comedians on this, however, and do not try out new material without testing it in front of others. If you were a comedian about to get your big break on national TV, you would not start or end with new material but with material you have used many times before with good results. You need to have total confidence in your closing comments or you can't pull it off. "If you're not 100 percent behind it you can't sell it," says comedian Orny Adams.

Display a quote

A quote from a famous figure can add credibility while summing up your message in a way a traditional summary slide cannot. The quote does not necessarily have to be from a famous person or a person known to the audience. The quote could be from one of your customers or even one of your children. The quote simply has to be evocative, provocative, or illustrative, and it needs to amplify the overall key message of the talk.

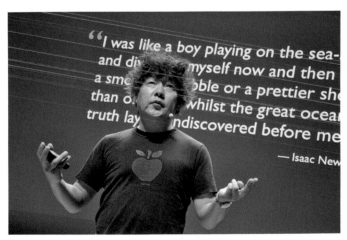

Brain scientist Ken Mogi presents clearly and passionately in front of a slide featuring a meaningful quote at TEDxTokyo 2010.

Pam Slim

Pam Slim is a well-known speaker, blogger, business consultant, and author of the best-selling book Escape from Cubicle Nation.

www.escapefromcubiclenation.com

Pam Slim offers good presentation advice for native English speakers who may be presenting to diverse, international crowds.

Speaking to an International Audience

These days, even the smallest-scale entrepreneur working out of her home office in Boise, Idaho, can have a circle of clients and partners from around the world. She may have an Australian graphic designer create her logo. She may manufacture her product line in China. She may hire technical developers and e-commerce experts from India. She may have customers from Bolivia and Belarus.

As a North American who has spent significant time living in different parts of the globe and working with large, multinational corporations, I would like to offer some tips for effective communication. A big part of presenting naked is allowing your audience to experience your true voice. Culturally irrelevant metaphors will cloud your message and make communication more difficult. To avoid that, keep the following things in mind for presentations and meetings:

1. Don't use baseball analogies when talking to a global audience.
Most people around the world know what baseball is. But it is not nearly as prevalent as football (aka "soccer") in most countries of the world. So if you are going to use a sports analogy, use one that most of your audience can relate to. I have felt very annoyed when hearing an executive address a global audience and use metaphors like "hitting it out of the park" or "throwing a curve ball." The rub is not that

the global audience will not understand, but that the executive did not take the time to think of a metaphor that is universally applicable.

2. Stay away from "country insider" metaphors and analogies.
My favorite is when a presenter talks about a business idea and says "but that is just motherhood and apple pie." If you are from the United States, you will nod your head in agreement since you know this means that the concept is wholesome and widespread. But if you are not from the United States, you may scratch your head and wonder how mothers and pies relate to business.

3. Speak clearly and enunciate.
This will benefit not only your audience members who speak English as a second language, but everyone else as well. A tip: If you smile while you talk, your words will come out clearer.

4. Plan for a level of interaction appropriate for the culture of your audience.
The first time I taught a class in Europe, I felt like a comedian playing a really hostile comedy club. I tend to be a very interactive presenter, and frequently ask the participants questions. Each question dropped like a lead weight in the room, and I was met by cool stares. At the break, I checked in with a colleague and was told that for this group in Amsterdam—with participants from England, France, Germany, Holland, and Switzerland—large group presentations were often more formal, and people would not speak up until they got in smaller groups. They looked to the instructor to be well prepared and knowledgeable, not to act as a talk show host.

Have them do something

Once I gave a talk on the importance of changing your state of mind as a way of coping with speaker's anxiety. To underscore the point of doing something physical as a way of changing your mental state, I had people stand up and jump with me to the music. This was right at the end. The energy of the room went through the roof and the smiles and laughter were contagious. You don't need to have people stand up and then jump up and down, but consider a way you can get them to move as long as it reinforces your message.

Make a call for action

Remember that the best presentations bring about change. Be clear, direct, and specific as you make your call for that change. For example, let's say the presentation was on strategies for maintaining a healthy weight. At the end, the presenter may say something like, "So tonight, before you go to bed, make a list of five ways you can change your lifestyle that will improve your health and give you more energy, then put that list on your refrigerator."

Inspire them

People do not want a pep rally, but everyone can appreciate a little inspiration. End on a positive note that gives people hope and encouragement to keep learning and investigating on their own. Inspiration is a positive and powerful emotion, and remember, you want people to *feel* something positive and powerful at the end of a talk. Inspiration is not the same thing as influence, of course, but do not underestimate the power of inspiration. Influence is measured over the long term. Good teachers, for example, influence students while also offering up encouragement and inspiration on a daily basis. Emotion in the form of inspiration moves people to make changes.

Naked Q&A Session

You do not have to include a Q&A session in a presentation, but if you do, it is generally at the end. This is acceptable, but be careful of ending your presentation by simply answering the last question—especially if the question was a bit off the actual point for which you want your presentation to be remembered. If your talk is long and has natural breaks, you can put Q&A sessions after each module, which may allow you to shorten or eliminate the Q&A section since you have been dealing with audience questions throughout the talk.

Even if you save questions and discussion for the end, make sure that, after you answer the final question, you take center stage again to close powerfully. One of the weakest ways to end a presentation goes something like this: "Well, that looks like all the time we have so I'll stop here. Thank you for your attention." A variation of this line has surely been repeated millions of times in boardrooms, conference halls, and classrooms across the globe.

Instead of asking if are there any more questions and hearing only crickets, be more assertive: "Right, we've only got time for one more. Who wants to ask the last question?" Alternatively, if you only have time for one more question, simply acknowledge someone who had their hand up previously but were not called on and say "Yes. Would you like to ask the last question, please?"

Just as with all other parts of the presentation, we must remain open, honest, transparent, and confident yet humble when dealing with questions. Here are a few things to keep in mind during your Q&A session.

• **Be engaging.** You have spent the entire presentation engaging and interacting with your audience, so do not act as if the presentation is already over. This is no time to phone it in. Keep your energy high and stay close to your audience.

• **Be brief.** Brevity is always appreciated as long as you are not being evasive. Get to your point and then move on.

• **Be silent.** When an audience member is speaking, do not interrupt once you think you understand the question. Let the questioner finish. Also, remember that it is OK to have a silent pause before you speak. Think about the question for a second. It's a conversation, not a race.

• **Be gracious.** You are still being judged by your audience. What you say matters—but people will remember how you dealt with people as well, especially if you are rude or impatient. "Naked" may mean casual and friendly, but it also means remaining always humble, gracious, and polite.

• **Be assertive.** Although you are friendly, casual, and open, you are also in charge. Don't let a long-winded person go on and on. You have a responsibility to the whole group to keep the discussion going.

• **Repeat or rephrase the question.** You show consideration for the whole room when you repeat an audience member's question for all to hear. This separates the pro from the beginner. Experienced presenters display their empathy for others and presence in the moment by repeating comments and questions so that all may hear. This also gives you a chance to make sure you correctly understand each question.

• **Ask questions in return.** You can also put questions to the audience. This is, after all, a conversation, so encourage people to participate.

• **Know when to stop.** Some of the key fundamental principles of judo include considering fully, acting decisively, and knowing when to stop. A good Q&A discussion period can be weakened if it goes on too long. If people really have burning questions or comments that did not get addressed, they will stay after your talk.

Lessons from Aikido

The modern Japanese martial art of aikido (合気道) has many lessons for us about dealing effectively with everyday challenging situations, including difficult questions and difficult people. *Aikido* means "the way of spiritual harmony" and was established in the 1920s by Morihei Ueshiba. Aikido is practiced in the dojo but it also teaches us everyday life applications of harmony and peace that expend far beyond the mat. Aikido is an effective response to conflict as well as an approach to living and way of life that seeks to promote harmonious solutions.

Morihei Ueshiba.

Ueshiba-sensei, also called O-sensei (the great teacher), was not a large man but his skills as a martial artist are said to be unparalleled. And as pointed out in John Steven's *Budo Secrets,* Ueshiba was also a philosopher and a very spiritual man who spent much time talking with his students about the deeper meanings reflected in Aikido. "The universe is always teaching us Aikido, though we fail to perceive it," Ueshiba said. O-sensei believed that the universe is our greatest teacher and our greatest friend. Aikido is nonviolent and stresses the concept of blending rather than opposing the force of another person or a situation. "The way of a warrior is not to kill and destroy but to foster life, to continually create," said Ueshiba. In aikido, one does not attack. "If you want to strike first to gain advantage over someone, this is proof your training is insufficient." Yet, one does not run or cower from attack either. Aikido is not passive. Rather, the aikidoka lets the other attack and uses the attacker's aggression or energy against him. In this way one can defeat an opponent through nonresistance by leveraging the other's force rather than one using his own brute strength to resist.

Here are seven practical lessons from the spirit of aikido that we can apply to communication in general and dealing with an aggressive audience member in particular.

1. Be here now.

In Life in Three Easy Lessons: Aikido, Harmony, and the Business of Living (Zanshin Press, 1997), Richard Moon calls the practice of being fully present and fully aware "Feel Where You Are." If you are to truly listen, engage, and empathize with someone challenging you, then you yourself must be completely aware of your situation, their situation, and all the subtle signals. One who is fully in the present cannot be caught off guard. "Feeling where you are," says Moon, "refines awareness into attention." Everyone in your audience deserves your full attention. There is energy in your presence, that is, when you are fully present.

2. Size matters not.

Aikido is not about brute strength. A well-trained Aikidoka can neutralize a much larger opponent, not by opposing his force, but by blending with the opponent's energy and guiding it, controlling it. You need not feel intimidated by the fact that others may prejudge you or assume you are in a weaker position. Perhaps you are new or young or an outsider, but these things do not matter. What matters is that you are prepared, ready, and fully listening—with your ears, and also with your eyes and your heart.

3. Strive for harmony.

Ki (気) can be translated as "life force" or "vital force" or more commonly as "spirit" or "energy." It is the living energy that flows through all things. Aikido teaches the student how to be in harmony with the spirit/energy of the universe and how to use this energy of life rather than resisting it. In Aikido, force and energy is not about strength of the body, which is limited, but about the power of ki, which is limitless. "We can't control ki but we can create the ideal situation within ourselves for ki to work," according to the late Aikido master Kensho Furuya. Proper mindfulness, stillness, and presence as well as relaxation of movement can help create the ideal situation for which this energy can flow.

4. Do not become defensive.

If an audience member is aggressive or even hostile toward you, do not react by being hostile back. This kind of resistance never works. When you allow stress (in the form of feelings related to defensiveness such as irritation, fear, impatience, and anger) your thinking becomes cloudy and your actions—including speaking—may become impulsive and foolish. Remember that we are not concerned with winning or losing, only with "true nature of things." During Q&A or discussion, we are interested in truth, just as our challenging questioner may be. If we are presenting truly naked with honesty, integrity, and good intention, we need not fear exposure since we have nothing to hide. We aim not to dominate people and situations. We are thinking more in terms of collaboration. By remaining calm, we can give measured responses instead of emotional reactions. "Impulsiveness and stubbornness give way to patience and understanding," says Moon, when we remain calm, focused, and centered.

5. Remain balanced.

Proper breathing is one crucial way to create the ideal situation for our ki to flow. Practice proper breathing at all times, but especially if your emotions try to kick in once you sense an attack. Become aware of your center. *Kikai tanden* is your body's center, located in your belly about three finger widths below your navel. This center is your inner compass. You must maintain good posture in which you are well-balanced physically and mentally. When dealing with a tough question, you should not be leaning to the side or have more weight on one foot than another. This imbalance can make you feel (and look) weaker on some level, although you may not be conscious of it. When you breathe, imagine that your breath is centered in the kikai tanden. Breathing from the kikai tanden is a common technique in many forms of meditation.

6. Do not regard others as the enemy.

Those who may challenge us are not the enemy. The only real enemy is inside us. O-sensei said, "I know not how to defeat others. I only know how to win over myself." O-sensei thwarted all attacks, but this preparedness was made possible through constant training and knowledge that the real enemies are fear, self-doubt, anger, confusion, and jealousy and other emotions inside us that can disturb the flow of ki. The key is to remember that "they" are never the enemy. Think instead in terms of mutual welfare and benefit. A key tenet of the martial arts is mutual respect for an opponent. In aikido, you can neutralize or deflect an attack by blending with the other's energy without causing harm to the opponent. If you think of your exchange as fighting, then you are resisting. Fighting is resisting and generating more conflict, which wastes energy and is ultimately fruitless. Fighting does not change minds or hearts.

7. Go with the flow.

This may sound to you like some groovy expression from the 1960s, but it is actually very practical. "Going with the flow" does not mean to act passively—quite the contrary. Going with the flow comes from a place of total awareness and an understanding of how things actually are in reality. Remember the universe and nature are our greatest teachers. The energy of a stream, for example, flows through the forest smoothly, having created its path around rocks and myriad natural obstacles. Or look how the bamboo in the same forest sways and bends in the wind but never breaks. When you remain calm and in harmony with your own personal state and the state of your surroundings, your natural energy can flow smoothly. But if you resist and push back from a place of stress and anger, your energy creates a discordance, leading to bad results for all concerned. In business and in life, attempts to make the other look foolish or engaging in ad hominem attacks is ignoble, unwise, and counterproductive.

There may be times, particularly during a Q&A session, when the line of questioning may seem especially challenging and even hostile. But there is no reason to feel intimidated. The only person who can get you off balance is yourself.

The slides below are a few of the ones used for an informal presentation on the issue of coping with tough questions and managing stress in difficult situations.

The real threat is not from others but from ourselves. In a presentation or meeting, we cannot control others, but we can work to remain balanced and steady. As Daisetsu Suzuki said, "There is harmony in our activity, and where there is harmony there is calmness." (Images in slides from iStockphoto.)

My life is my message.

— Mahatma Gandhi

In Sum

• When your ideas and energy are transferred to others and cause them to make a change, we can say that your message has resonance. However, sustaining a connection until the end of a presentation and delivering a powerful finish requires that you understand your audience well.

• The ideas and messages that stick best contain six common elements: Simplicity, Unexpectedness, Concreteness, Credibility, Emotions, and Stories. The stickier your message and delivery at the end, the more likely your messages will be remembered and acted upon.

• However you choose to deliver your closing, do not retreat from the audience—get close to them. End on a positive note that gives people hope and encouragement to keep learning and investigating on their own.

• Even if you save questions and discussion for the end, make sure that, after you answer the final question, you take center stage again to close powerfully.

My friend, drop all your preconceived and fixed ideas and be neutral. Do you know why this cup is useful? Because it is empty.

— Bruce Lee

7

Continuous Improvement Through Persistence

The concept of gambaru (頑張る) is deeply embedded in the Japanese culture and approach to life. The literal meaning of *gambaru* expresses the idea of sticking with a task with tenacity until it is completed—of making a persistent effort until success is achieved. The imperative form, "gambette," is used very often in daily language to encourage others to "do your best" in work, to "fight on!" and "never give up!" during a sporting event or studying for an exam. Persistence is also reflected in the old Buddhist saying, "In the confrontation between the stream and the rock, the stream always wins—not through strength, but through persistence." There is a strong belief in education and business in Japan that great improvement can be achieved by anyone, as long as they never give up and put forth a great effort that is sincere. Success does not have to be fast—what's more important is that one simply does their absolute best and remains persistent.

Although Japanese culture may place a special emphasis on continuous effort, the importance of persistence in achieving one's goals is obviously not confined to Japan. Renowned psychologist Edward De Bono, for example, has noted that in his vast experience, those who have become successful have two major qualities: (1) they expected to do well, and (2) they were persistent. "The one thing that all successful people have in common is persistence," says De Bono. "They keep going and regard setbacks as minor inconveniences. If you keep going you will get there." Intrinsic motivation is the driving force of persistence. *New York Times* best-selling author Daniel Pink also identifies persistence as a key aptitude that sets people apart. In his career guide called *The Adventures of Johnny Bunko* (Riverhead Trade, 2008), Pink says that while talent is obviously important, persistence, more often than not, trumps talent. "The more intrinsic motivation you have, the more likely you are to persist. The more you persist, the more likely you are to succeed." Our techniques and approach may change over time, but embracing the gambaru spirit means keeping our goals clear and focused. "Persistence isn't using the same tactics over and over," says bestselling author and entrepreneur Seth Godin. "That's just annoying. Persistence is having the same goal over and over."

Through persistence, the gentle stream will not be stopped. Be like the stream.

Lessons Are Everywhere

Excellence in presentation and public speaking is something virtually anyone can achieve with persistence. Yet, the art of dynamic presentation as a skill to be studied and acquired is given little attention in formal educational settings. Academic classes and seminars that explore the art of storytelling and creating structured narratives for the world outside of the arts—and designing high-impact visuals to amplify those narratives—largely do not exist. But that's OK, because you can make vast improvements outside the world of formal education by taking it upon yourself to learn what is not taught in schools.

Anyone who is successful in business and in life continues his or her education long after leaving school. The Japanese call lifelong learning *shogai gakushu* (生涯学習). The spirit of shogai gakushu is that personal growth and learning should continue until the day you die. There is no end to improvement. The idea of intrinsically motivated, persistent self-education has always been important. In the connected digital world of today, it has never been easier to gain access to resources and materials—many or which are very cheap or even free—from all over the world. There are no longer any excuses for torturing your audiences and coworkers with mind-numbing death-by-PowerPoint presentations or dull, dispassionate speeches because you don't know another way. The examples of people who present differently and effectively and naked are everywhere. I point to many of them on my web site: **www.presentationzen.com**.

Everyone Can Improve

Bill Gates is a man with a big heart and a big brain. I'm a huge fan. Yet, in spite of all his many talents and contributions, delivering effective presentations—especially if slides are involved—has never been one of his strong points. Even former Apple CEO Gil Amelio noted in 1998 that Gates "does not take well to standing at the podium." Things, started to change, however, in early 2009. When I attended TED in Long Beach that year, I witnessed an engaging presentation by Bill Gates. Even his visuals were better than the usual cluttered and bullet point-filled slides (although they still had a ways to go). In October 2009, we began to see much more improvement in Gates's delivery—especially in his visuals.

In a presentation in Washington, D.C., in the fall of 2009, Bill and Melinda Gates gave an engaging presentation with wonderfully designed, high-impact visuals to explain why they are "impatient optimists." Their presentation employed a good mix of data and real examples to make the case that the world is getting better, but (1) not fast enough, and (2) not for everyone. That's what they mean by "impatient optimists." With the help of clear visuals and video clips, the Gates's did an effective job of showing the good news about how real people have been transformed.

Bill Gates showed even further improvement in his presentation on energy at the 2010 TED Conference. There, he used logic, reason, structure, and a bit of humor. He stated the problem, the challenges, some possible solutions—and went into just a little detail on one example, using the storytelling technique of zooming in on the particular to illuminate the general. Gates's visuals were simple, clear, and high impact.

Gates is one of the most powerful, richest men in the world, and yet even he made an effort to change and become a much more effective, natural, engaging presenter. When you're trying to change the world, your presentations better be remarkable.

You must empty your cup

To learn to present differently in a more naked style, you first need to drop the old habits and rules that have been holding you back. There is an old, often-told story of a Japanese Zen master who was visited by a university professor who came inquiring about the meaning of Zen. First, the master began to serve him tea. The master poured his visitor's cup full, and then kept on pouring. The visitor watched the overflowing cup silently until he could no longer restrain himself. "It is overfull. No more will go in!" the visiting professor shouted. "Like this cup," the master replied, "you too are full of your own opinions and speculations. How can I show you Zen unless you first empty your cup?"

Indeed, if we approach life with a full cup, we cannot learn anything new. New skills, new approaches, and different ways of thinking will be blocked. Wild ideas, crazy notions, and remarkable insights will have no space to enter a world of certainty, pride, overconfidence, and commitment to the past and the known. Part of emptying our cup is a willingness to unlearn what we think we know to be the best or only way. As a wise old Jedi master once said in a galaxy far, far away, "You must unlearn what you have learned."

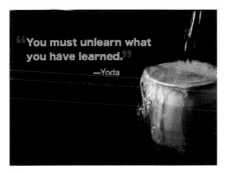

Slide combines idea of unlearning and emptying your cup. (Image from iStockphoto.)

Presentation (and Life) Lessons from the Dojo

Kyuzo Mifune (1883–1965) is considered one of the great judo masters of the modern era. Though Mifune was not physically large, even in his old age he could defeat much larger and younger men. According to John Stevens in *Budo Secrets,* Mifune often used a technique called kuki-nage (air throw), which is based on the principle  of a perfect sphere. "A sphere never loses its center, it moves swiftly without strain, and it does not resist force." The meaning of the term *judo* (柔道) is gentle + way or "The way of gentleness." A key tenet of judo is that the soft controls the hard, that one can be successful by adapting to constantly changing circumstances and using the opponent's force against himself.

Kyuzo Mifune's seven rules of judo practice are written for those who practice the martial art of judo. Yet you can use your imagination to see how these simple rules can serve as invaluable guides in your life and work outside the dojo. You can certainly see the applications to public speaking and leadership. For example, a sure way to lose credibility in front of most business audiences is to make light of your competition by saying disparaging things about them. True humility is a sign of strength, overconfidence or arrogance is a sign of weakness. Take some time to think about these seven rules as they relate to your own life and work.

1. Do not make light of an opponent.
2. Do not lose self-confidence.
3. Maintain good posture.
4. Develop speed.
5. Project power in all directions.
6. Develop self-control.
7. Never stop training.

There are no quick fixes or secret techniques

Whether we are talking about business, presentations, or life in general, there are no panaceas to the challenges we face. There is no substitute for study, steady practice, and a commitment to continuous improvement. For this point, too, judo has a lesson for all of us. "Do not place hope in finding a secret technique," said Kyuzo Mifune. "Polish the mind through ceaseless training; that is the key to effective techniques."

You have to believe it

One of the more memorable scenes in *Star Wars V* is when Yoda uses the Force to effortlessly free Luke Skywalker's x-wing fighter from the bog. Luke was naturally shocked by this feat and said, "I don't, I don't believe it." To which Yoda responded with a heavy sigh and these simple words: "That is why you fail." The easy thing to do is the normal thing to do. Bringing a more natural approach to your communication in general and your presentations in particular involves risks—once you are allowing yourself to be exposed, transparent, and naked. You may not always succeed, but you must believe in yourself and your own approach. Belief is not a sufficient condition for success, but it's a necessary one.

It's all up to you

Famed author and professor Isaac Asimov once said that "Self-education is, I firmly believe, the only kind of education there is." I think the spirit of this statement is perfect for our times. Yes, of course teachers are important and formal education is necessary. But most knowledge and skills gained over the course of a lifetime result from our personal persistence to seek out knowledge, information, and good examples that we can use to educate ourselves. Self-education is the key to continuous, lifelong improvement.

Knowledge and inspiration are everywhere for those who are persistent. (Image in slide by iStockphoto.)

Naturalness and the Three Cs of Presenting with Impact

The theme of this book is that naturalness in delivery—bringing more of your own unique personality to your presentations—will amplify your messages in a way that will get them noticed, understood, and remembered. You can think about this in terms of three Cs: Contribution, Connection, Change.

• **Contribution.** Some people think that a presentation or an invitation to speak is a burden or, at best, an obligation that can't be avoided. This is the wrong attitude. Instead, think of presentation as a welcome opportunity to make a difference. Every presentation or speech is a chance to make a contribution. We all live for the opportunity to contribute—it's what makes us human. A contribution is never about us—it's always about them. We show respect for the audience by being well prepared. We show we care by sharing a bit of ourselves and a small part of our own humanity. Do not allow yourself to get bogged down in a haze of self-doubt and worry about whether or not you are good enough. To win or to lose is not the point. The conductor of the Boston Philharmonic Orchestra and presenter extraordinaire Benjamin Zander says something similar while encouraging one of his talented students: "We are about contribution. That's what our job is. It's not about impressing people. It's not about getting the next job. It's about contributing something." We can apply this spirit to the art of presentation as well.

• **Connection.** To contribute and share, we have to make a solid connection with others in the room. Where there is no connection, there can be no contribution. If we can make a solid and lasting connection with others, then we create the space for our contribution to be heard and take root.

• **Change.** Through contribution we make a difference—we make a difference because we change things. Sometimes the change is big and sometimes the change is virtually imperceptible—but it's real all the same. It is the positive change that results from an honest, transparent contribution in the moment. These tiny contributions in the aggregate are what keep humanity moving forward.

Create art and make change

I've always said that presentation is more art than science. So what is art? In a recent interview with David Siteman Garland, Seth Godin said this about art in the context of work: "Art is a generous action—it's when a human connects to another human and makes a change." The work that we do *could* be art, but if we are just following the rules, playing it safe, and sort of working-by-the-numbers (as in paint-by-numbers), then the work lacks connection and difference, and therefore lacks art. The best presentations are works of art (in a sense) because the best presenters connect in the spirit of contribution and generosity and help people make a change. The worst presentations and speeches are the usual ones, the ones that are perfunctory, routine, safe, and utterly forgettable. Nobody ever got fired for doing the expected and the safe—at least not in the old world. But it's a new world now. And the professionals who are remarkable and who want to make a difference—teachers, doctors, engineers, aid workers, and businesspeople of all types—are the ones who create art. Today, more than ever, there are opportunities to speak in front of others to make a connection and contribute to lasting change—that is, to create art.

You had it once. You can have it again.

Pablo Picasso once said, "All children are born artists. The problem is to remain artists as we grow up." The Japanese are not known for producing many remarkable orators or engaging presenters. Yet when I visit elementary schools in Japan, I find the students there are always amazingly engaged, energetic, and happy to share their ideas and stories. I suspect elementary schools in your town are filled with similarly energetic, hopeful students as well.

As very young children, we were naturally authentic communicators and conversationalists. But then somewhere down the line we began to be guided away from that natural, human talent as a shift occurred in our education that emphasized "the correct answer" and demanded careful, formal speech—speech that did not encourage engagement and dissuaded our true personalities from coming out lest we run the risk of ridicule. But you are an adult now and you can change your destiny. You can find again that naturalness, creativity, and energy you had as a child and combine it with your knowledge, skills, and passion to make real human-to-human connections that lead to remarkable change.

"When there is no crookedness in one's heart, we say that one is natural and childlike."
— Daisetz T. Suzuki

"Nana korobi, ya oki."
(Fall down seven times,
get up eight times.)

— Japanese proverb

In Sum

• To learn to present differently in a more naked style, you first need to drop the old habits and rules that have been holding you back.

• Naturalness in delivery—bringing more of your own unique personality to your presentations—will amplify your messages in a way that will get them noticed, understood, and remembered. You can think about this in terms of three Cs: Contribution, Connection, Change.

• The best presentations are works of art (in a sense) because the best presenters connect in the spirit of contribution and generosity and help people make a change.

Contact:
info@garrreynolds.com
www.presentationzen.com

Index

your world. our stock.

We've seen a lot in ten years.

Whether you're a designer, advertiser, entrepreneur or blogger, we can help you tell your story with royalty-free photos, illustrations, video and audio. Say anything with iStockphoto.

15 free images & 20% off 50 credits or more:
iStockphoto.com/nakedpresentation

iStockphoto